HORSES

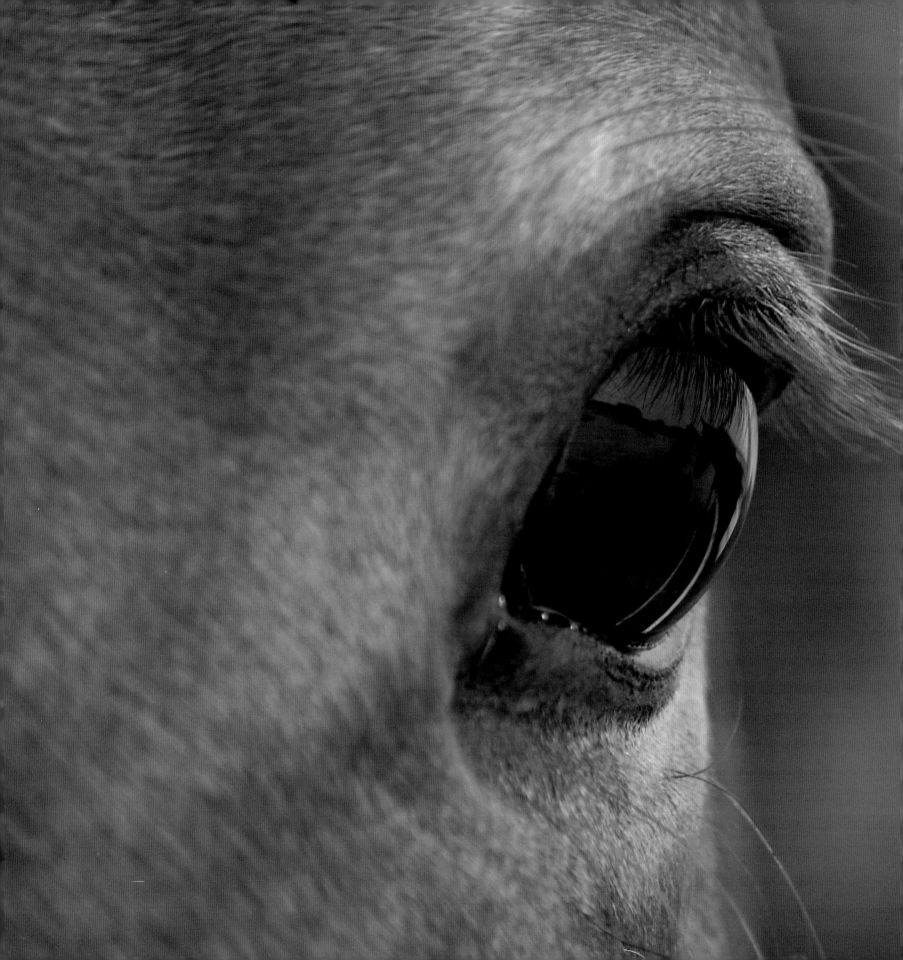

HORSES

SCHOLASTIC

Turkestan pack saddle 1871

CONTENTS

FOREWORD

The graceful animals we call horses are a superb combination of power and beauty. For thousands of years, people have worked closely with these magnificent animals on the farm, the battlefield, the racecourse, and the show ring.

Horses influence our lives sometimes without our knowing it. Daily, around the world, there are workhorses pulling carts carrying goods that we need, laboring on the farm to produce the food we eat, or working in the forests to provide timber for our homes. Horse characters have captured hearts and minds for generations, starring in books, TV series, and movies, from *Black Beauty* to *Flicka*, *Seabiscuit*, *War Horse*, and *Free Rein*.

As a horse lover, perhaps you are lucky enough to own a horse or pony or ride one regularly; maybe you simply dream of owning one. As well as fascinating facts about breeds that are old favorites, this book will introduce you to breeds you have not yet met, and you will be amazed, inspired, and informed as you turn the pages.

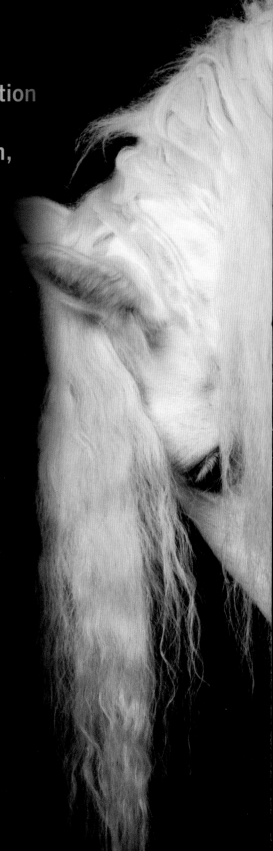

Horses are a wonderful combination of strength and beauty, as can be seen in this picture of a powerful gray draft horse with its head shrouded in a glorious mane.

A SPECIAL BOND

The relationship between humans and horses is unique and powerful. There is a bond that develops between many horses and their riders, sometimes over a period of months or years. They tune into each other's physical and mental ways, and they form a partnership that is unlike any other. The horse not only lets the rider sit on its back and guide it, but it chooses to do so, an expression of supreme trust and confidence.

INSTINCT FOR TRUST

In the wild, horses are very social and family-oriented. In a herd, there is typically a lead stallion and mare that keep the rest moving and safe, and each horse depends on the rest for protection. Relationships within the herd hold it together and ensure that the horses survive in the toughest of conditions. Bonds develop between members of the group as they spend time in their daily routine to groom each other. When a horse is domesticated, this instinct for trust and reliance is easily developed between a horse and its owner if the horse is well-treated and looked after.

OWNING A HORSE

There are things that must be put in place to ensure that the way that a horse relates to its owner is of benefit to both parties.

Safe ride for royalty
Two royal children ride in pannier basket chairs on the back of a pony. Their mother, Alexandra (standing), was wife to Queen Victoria's eldest son, and later became queen consort when her husband became Britain's King Edward VII.

Firstly, the horse needs safe and warm stabling. Secondly, it is important to figure out a balanced diet, with the right amount of foodstuff for the energy the horse needs. Thirdly, from the start, it is vital to provide the correct and thoughtful training for whatever you want the horse to do. And last, but not least, you need to make sure the horse has enough exercise, both by letting it run free in the pasture, or by taking it out for a daily ride. If the horse is healthy and happy, you will reap the rewards of being a horse owner.

FOR THE LOVE OF HORSES

If it is not possible for you to own a horse or pony, but you still love watching them, you can visit the local stables for a ride, or enjoy a day out at the races or at a dressage competition. You can read books about horses, watch films, or take a virtual ride on the internet. Horses are magnificent animals at one with nature. They have a great deal to offer, and any contact with them can only be of benefit.

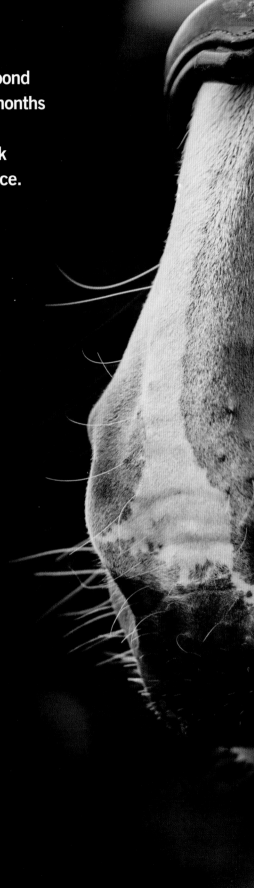

Hunting pony
In western Mongolia, a Kazakh woman mounted on a Tibetan pony hunts hares using a trained golden eagle. This is an ancient and traditional way of hunting that dates back 4,000 years.

A lasting relationship
Many horses today live to be over 30 years old, although some live even longer—in 2012, an Irish Draft crossbreed called Shayne died at the ripe old age of 51! Owning a horse is therefore a longterm commitment that should not be undertaken lightly. However, if the horse has been well kept, and the proper attention given to feed, as well as dental and hoof care, horses are a joy to be around, even when they are fully retired and can no longer be ridden.

REFINING THE BREED

Over time, a variety of uses for the horse developed and breeding for particular traits and skills became increasingly important. And as breeders discovered how to refine and target the breeding, a variety of other professions came into being to support this sometimes demanding profession—lads for racing, vets, and therapists among others.

Bred to trot
In harness racing, horses pull a two-wheeled vehicle called a sulky at a trot round the racetrack, like these riders who are competing at the hippodrome in Palma, Mallorca. In the 1800s, breeders selected horses that could trot or pace a mile (1.6 km) within the "standard" time of 2 minutes and 30 seconds to develop the Standardbred Trotter.

The breeding of horses goes back thousands of years. As a greater demand for the horse to do different tasks increased, so did the development of the number of breeds. For example, when stronger horses were needed for farm work, to carry knights in armor, or to pull large weights, heavier breeds were created. And people began to learn that they needed not only to develop new breeds but also conserve existing ones.

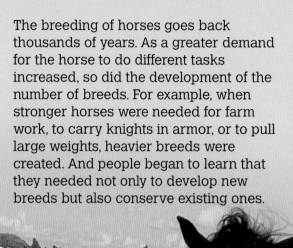

PEDIGREES

A horse's or pony's character and traits reflect generations of ancestors. The selection of those ancestors by breeders is what is recorded in their pedigree, a family tree that tells interested parties all about the horse's bloodlines. The selection of bloodlines is what a breeder uses to predict whether a horse will be a racer, a performer, or suitable for future breeding stock. An experienced breeder will recognize names of horses and breeders in the ancestors and that will help them to identify the horse they are looking for. For example, Quarter Horses names to look out for may be Bar, Zip, and Peppy.

TARGETED BREEDING

Around the world, there are stud farms that specialize in the breeding of quality horses. For many, this is a million-dollar business, with some horses being transported great distances to other countries to

Ancient horses

About 4.5 million years ago, two kinds of horses began to develop in the wild. One branch gave rise to other equines including mules and asses, while the other developed into the modern horse. Przewalski's horse *(right)* is the only survivor of four types of primitive horse that existed 10,000 years ago.

breed. Today, these animals and any others used for breeding have to be inspected before they satisfy the standard for a particular breed and can be registered in a stud book. Some even have to do performance trials. These controls exist to preserve the quality of the breed and make sure that all the horses share similar characteristics.

In some cases, breeds threatened with extinction have been restored because of measures taken by dedicated breeders. For example, Przewalski's horse has been reintroduced to China, Mongolia, and Kazakhstan and the population is increasing, moving its status from "critically endangered" to "endangered."

Early days

Horse racing has been an increasingly popular sport for more than 200 years. These jockeys are pictured at Doncaster racecourse, England, in 1814. The world's oldest classic horse race, the St. Leger, is still run today at this racecourse.

ABOUT THE HORSE

To look after a horse you need to understand it. That means that, as well as finding out about its ancestry, you need to establish that it has a good shape and structure, and that it is suitable for the work you want it to do—for example, a riding horse or pony has to be strong enough to carry its rider. Then you can begin to build a strong, long-lasting relationship.

GROWING UP

For the first year of its life, a horse or pony is called a foal, and from 12–24 months it is described as a yearling. Horses and ponies can continue to grow until they are five or six years old. Until they reach this age their bones are not strong enough for hard work.

As horses and ponies age, their coat may change color. Most foals are born pale, sometimes with light-colored eyes and pinkish skin. This paleness helps to camouflage them from predators. Most young horses shed their baby coats around the age of one, and then darker colors take over. The exceptions are the grays, which are mostly born dark, then become lighter until they are almost white.

CONFORMATION

A horse or pony's conformation is a way of describing its shape and structure. This varies from breed to breed—draft horses will be powerful but stocky, while racehorses will be streamlined and longer-legged. In either case, the horse's body should have a good bone structure and musculature, and its different parts should be in proportion. A horse's conformation has an effect on how the horse moves and jumps.

Points of a horse
The visible parts of a horse's anatomy are called the points. You need to study these and be aware of any changes that might signal the need for you to take action, such as getting a vet to take a look.

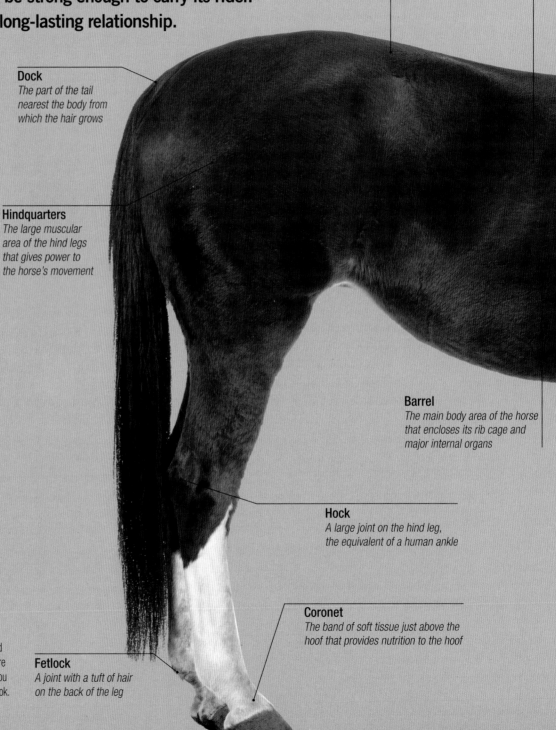

Flank
Where the hind legs and the barrel meet

Back
A deep-laid spine with the major back muscle running along its left and right side

Dock
The part of the tail nearest the body from which the hair grows

Hindquarters
The large muscular area of the hind legs that gives power to the horse's movement

Barrel
The main body area of the horse that encloses its rib cage and major internal organs

Hock
A large joint on the hind leg, the equivalent of a human ankle

Coronet
The band of soft tissue just above the hoof that provides nutrition to the hoof

Fetlock
A joint with a tuft of hair on the back of the leg

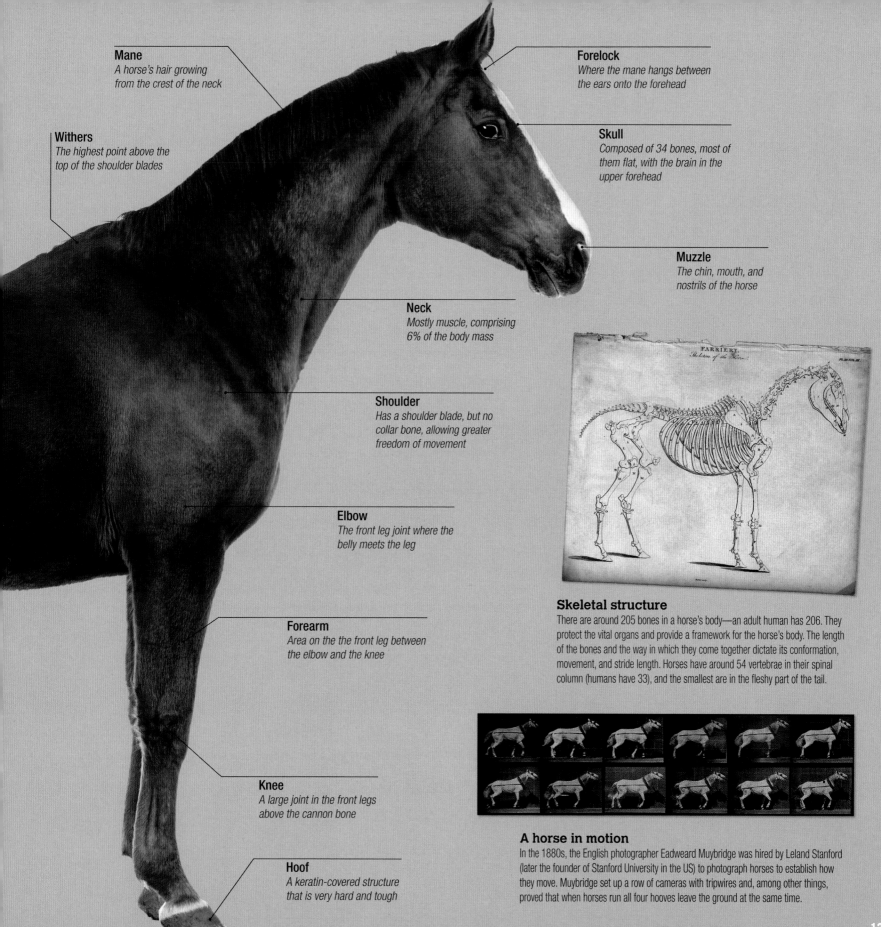

Mane
*A horse's hair growing
from the crest of the neck*

Forelock
*Where the mane hangs between
the ears onto the forehead*

Withers
*The highest point above the
top of the shoulder blades*

Skull
*Composed of 34 bones, most of
them flat, with the brain in the
upper forehead*

Muzzle
*The chin, mouth, and
nostrils of the horse*

Neck
*Mostly muscle, comprising
6% of the body mass*

Shoulder
*Has a shoulder blade, but no
collar bone, allowing greater
freedom of movement*

Elbow
*The front leg joint where the
belly meets the leg*

Skeletal structure

There are around 205 bones in a horse's body—an adult human has 206. They protect the vital organs and provide a framework for the horse's body. The length of the bones and the way in which they come together dictate its conformation, movement, and stride length. Horses have around 54 vertebrae in their spinal column (humans have 33), and the smallest are in the fleshy part of the tail.

Forearm
*Area on the the front leg between
the elbow and the knee*

Knee
*A large joint in the front legs
above the cannon bone*

A horse in motion

In the 1880s, the English photographer Eadweard Muybridge was hired by Leland Stanford (later the founder of Stanford University in the US) to photograph horses to establish how they move. Muybridge set up a row of cameras with tripwires and, among other things, proved that when horses run all four hooves leave the ground at the same time.

Hoof
*A keratin-covered structure
that is very hard and tough*

LIGHT

HORSES

Great companions

Horses are highly social herd animals. They communicate with each other through body language as well as by making neighing or whinnying sounds to show emotion or warn of danger. Within each herd there is a pecking order, with certain horses exerting dominance, and this herd instinct is what makes so many light horses such willing workers and great rides for people.

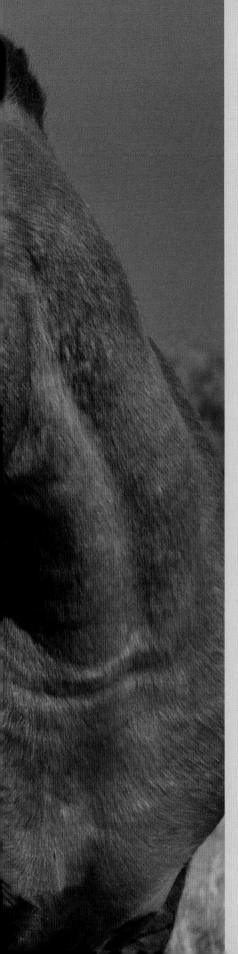

THE EVERYDAY HORSES

The greatest number of horses bred today are light horses. They are used mainly for riding and shows, although some do light work and driving. Light horses are split into two groups—hotblood and warmblood—depending on their characteristics and ancestry.

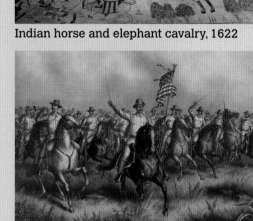

Indian horse and elephant cavalry, 1622

Hotblood and warmblood horses have very different temperaments. The hotbloods, such as the Arabian (the oldest breed of all) and the Thoroughbred, are spirited, nervous, and full of energy. They need very careful training and handling, but their lighter bodies and passionate nature make them excellent racing horses, and their speed outstrips all the other breeds.

Warmbloods, on the other hand, are crossbred hot- and cold-blooded horses. This results in breeds that are gentler, calmer, and eager to please. They make wonderful riding horses for all ages, are used as workhorses and for trail riding, and they are also successful in competition.

Smaller than the powerful draft horses, and larger than most ponies, light horses have small bones and are lean-legged. The large variety of warmblood breeds produces horses that excel in many different ways.

Carriage horses
Light horses have always made good driving horses, whether they were pulling a stagecoach across the Wild West in America, or an elegant carriage to the opera house in Rome, Italy.

American cavalry charge, Cuba, 1898

Great warmblood riding horses include the American Saddlebred and the Morgan. Heavier, muscled light horses, such as the Quarter Horse and Appaloosa, are often used to work on ranches. Breeds such as the Dutch Warmblood, Hanoverian, and Trakehner are sports horses that excel in many competitions, including dressage, show jumping, and eventing. Some light horses, such as the Tennessee Walking Horse, are bred for an exceptionally smooth ride. These gaited, or "gentlemen's horses" move like other horses do at a walk, but move each of their legs independently, keeping one foot on the ground at all times. This means there is no bounce and therefore less stress to the rider. The horses use less energy, which gives them more stamina and an ability to travel long distances. Some of them walk so fast that even a trotting horse cannot keep up.

Horse-drawn carts in Turkey, 1922

> **"**When **I bestride** him, **I soar**, I am **a hawk**: he **trots the air** . . .**"**
> *Henry V*, William Shakespeare

A dressage competition, Russia, 2017

FERAL HORSES

There are no truly wild horses left in the world today. Horses known as feral are free-ranging animals descended from domesticated stock. They live in a wide range of habitats, from islands and deserts to grasslands and forests.

Feral horses are found in many countries around the world, but Australia has the largest population—around 400,000. Most live in small herds of around 5 to 12 horses, with one stallion, several mares, and their foals. When the male horses are two years old, they leave the herd and form a herd with other young males.

In some parts of the world, horses and ponies are also found living in semi-feral conditions. These are privately owned and are rounded up each year for health checks, or to have foals selected for sale either for commercial reasons or to avoid the population getting too large. For example, more than 70,000 wild horses are currently living on the public lands of the American West, which some say is only capable of supporting 27,000 animals, and there is a debate about how to manage this situation. On the other hand, semi-feral ponies are often introduced to wild places such as heathland to keep the plants there healthy and diverse.

A band of feral Mustangs in the western United States

Semi-feral Konik horses in a nature reserve in the Netherlands

Small but tough

Przewalski's horses have to be tough and adaptable to cope with the extreme conditions found in Mongolia. Temperatures can soar to 104°F (40°C) in the Gobi Desert in the summer, and dip as low as −49°F (−45°C) on the steppes in the depths of winter.

PRZEWALSKI'S HORSE

CENTRAL ASIAN FERAL HORSE

The endangered Przewalski's horse is the world's last remaining truly feral horse. Once found throughout Europe and Asia, changes in the environment and competition with people caused their disappearance in the wild by the 1960s. However, successful breeding in captivity has led to the reintroduction of Przewalski's horses into parts of Mongolia, although their numbers are still very low.

Breed name: Przewalski's horse

Other names: Mongolian wild horse, Dzungarian horse

Breed purpose: wild population

Breed size: 12–14 hands

Coat color: dun

Place of origin: western Mongolia and northern China

Ancestors: probably sub-species of a wild horse, possibly the now-extinct tarpan

Russian explorer
Mikolaj Przewalski (1839–1888) was a Russian geographer who explored Central Asia in the late 19th century, journeying through China, Mongolia, and regions unknown to the West. On his travels, he saw and described various previously unknown animal species, including the horse that was named after him.

Mongolians call Przewalski's horse *takhi*, which means "**spirit**" or "**worthy of worship**."

Herd life
Living in small family units, each group is made up of a handful of mares and foals and one stallion. The dominant mare controls where they graze and the stallion defends the herd against predators. Younger males live in bachelor groups.

A family group of Przewalski's horses

Solid build
These horses are small and stocky, with short legs, plumed tails, and dark lower legs.

Bristly mane
Their coats are dun-colored with dark, zebralike manes, large heads, and thick necks.

Mother and foal

Born to run
With food and water sometimes scarce in Mongolia's harsh conditions, the family groups are constantly on the move in their search for something to eat and drink. For this reason, it is crucial that foals can stand and walk within an hour of being born.

MUSTANG

FERAL HORSE OF THE AMERICAN WEST

This classic horse of the American West is a wild descendant of horses carried to the Americas by the Spanish conquistadores in the 16th century. The name "Mustang" comes from the Spanish *mestengo*, meaning "stray." And they did stray—by the end of the 19th century there were up to two million mustangs running wild in the western US.

Breed name: Mustang

Other name: Spanish Mustang

Breed purpose: riding, packhorse

Size: 15 hands

Coat color: any color, but mostly bay, black, chestnut, gray and brown, palomino

Place of origin: North America

Ancestors: Andalusian, Arabian, Barb, Lusitano

Name takers
The wild image of the Mustang has been adopted by people to describe their inventions. The popular 1960s Ford Mustang car with its running horse emblem was sure to grab the imagination of its buyer by reflecting the smooth, fleet movements of its feral inspiration.

A typical large mustang herd traveling across the plains of central America

A special relationship
Before Europeans introduced the horse to the Americas, Native Americans had never seen an animal like it. It was not long, however, before many tribes learned how to catch and tame these feral horses, using them to transport goods, run down bison, and later, as war horses, to fight against the forcible taking of their territories.

Stallions fight each other for a mare

Herd life
Each large herd has one stallion and around eight females and their young, and is led by a mare and a stallion over six years in age. Herds can join together if threatened. Mustangs can live for up to 40 years.

Mustangs are allowed to **run free** on **34 million acres** (138 million hectares) of **public land** in the **US**.

Bright eyes
Below the broad forehead, the wide spaced eyes can be brown or sometimes blue, gray, or green.

Thick mane
The short neck is covered with a flowing mane and forelock, a first protection against flies.

Slender muzzle
The long, narrow face leads down to a small muzzle with large nostrils.

Hindquarters
The horse has a short back with a steep, sloping croup that indicates muscular strength in the hindquarters to aid jumping.

Legs and hooves
These are particularly strong, having developed over centuries of roaming the rocky terrain in the western United States.

Tail carriage
Unlike its thoroughbred ancestors, the Mustang has a tail that is low set with a long skirt.

A mixed breed
As a result of their checkered history of cross-breeding from Andalusian, Lusitano, Arab, and Barb horses, the characteristics of Mustangs are very varied. However, they are all short, muscular, and hardy—intelligent horses built for survival. They graze on grasses, and eat around 5–6 lbs (2.3–2.7 kg) a day.

Coat colors
Mustangs can be any color, and their face markings and coat patterns are striking. Solid colors include bay, chestnut, and gray.

Pinto

Red roan

Bay

Appaloosa

Running free

In the south of France is a large delta where the Rhône meets the Mediterranean Sea—France's "Wild West." Known as the Camargue, this is a 360-sq. mile (930-sq. km) area of marshy wetland, salt flats, and red salt lagoons that is home to herds of free-roaming Camargue horses. One of the oldest breeds in the world, the Camargue (*see p.26*) are today bred and trained in farms along the river and coastline, but the gray-coated adults run free most of the year.

BRUMBY

AUSTRALIA

Brumbies are the descendants of horses brought by European settlers to Australia from the 18th century onward. These include many horses that escaped from mining settlements during the 1851 Gold Rush. Wild herds grew rapidly and today Australia has around 300,000 Brumbies, many of them in the Northern Territory.

Breed name: Brumby

Other name: n/a

Breed purpose: none

Size: 14–15 hands

Coat color: all colors

Place of origin: Australia

Ancestors: various

Outback vandal?

These tough feral horses live in large herds and have adapted well to the harsh environment of the Australian outback. Some people have accused the brumbies of damaging the habitat by overgrazing, trampling on vegetation, and chewing on tree bark. Others say brumbies help keep tracks and trails clear.

CAMARGUE

FRANCE

Camargue horses live in isolated herds in the wetlands of the Camargue in southern France (*see pp.24–25*). Known as the "horses of the sea," they are often seen wading through water or galloping on the beach. In the 1970s, the breed was also introduced to the Po Delta in Italy.

Breed name: Camargue

Other name: n/a

Breed purpose: cattle work

Size: 13–14.2 hands

Coat color: gray

Place of origin: Camargue, France

Ancestors: possibly the extinct Solutre horse; Spanish, Portuguese, North African breeds

Sturdy horses of the sea

All adult Camargue horses are gray. They have a stocky build and are exceptionally hardy, living on tough plants and reeds. During festivals in the Camargue, some of the wild horses are ridden by local *guardians*, who use them to round up bulls and drive them through the streets.

Cowboys known as *guardians* riding Camargue horses

Herd of Camargue horses in Italy

Distinctive looks

The Losino has a large head, big, expressive eyes, and thick lips. It has a broad back with a low-set tail, and a long thick coat of hair, especially in the winter.

Breed name: Losino
Other names: Caballo Losino or Caballo de Raza Losina
Breed purpose: pack horses
Size: 15 hands
Coat color: black
Place of origin: northern Spain
Ancestors: local breeds including the Pottock, Garrano, extinct Catalan

LOSINO

NORTHERN SPAIN

The Losino horse gets its name from the Losa Valley in northern Spain where it was first bred. By 1986, there were only 30 Losinos left as a result of extensive farming and cross-breeding with other horses and donkeys.

LAVRADEIRO

NORTHERN BRAZIL

These wild horses live in Roraima in northern Brazil, close to the border with Venezuela. They are descended from Spanish and Portuguese horses that were brought over in the 16th century by Europeans during the conquest of South America. Today, they are very rare, and numbers in 2010 ranged between just 1,260 and 1,680.

Breed name: Lavradeiro
Other name: n/a
Breed purpose: herding livestock
Size: 11–12 hands

Coat colors: brown, dark gray, sorrel, bay
Place of origin: Roraima, northern Brazil
Ancestors: Arabian, Barb, Andalusian

Sturdy build

The Misaki is small and dark-colored. Its head is large compared with the rest of its body, which is short and stocky. It is believed to be descended from horses brought over from China at various times to be used as pack horses or for warfare.

Breed name: Misaki
Other name: n/a
Breed purpose: pack horses
Size: 13–14.2 hands
Coat color: black, bay
Place of origin: Kyushu, Japan
Ancestors: unknown

MISAKI

KYUSHU, JAPAN

This small feral horse can be found grazing on Cape Toi on the island of Kyushu in Japan. In the 1970s, there were only about 50 left in the wild, but numbers have now increased to about 120.

Breed name: Namib Desert Horse
Other name: n/a
Breed purpose: unknown
Size: 14–15 hands
Coat color: bay, chestnut, brown
Place of origin: Namib Desert, Namibia
Ancestors: domestic horses abandoned in the 1920s

NAMIB DESERT HORSE

NAMIBIA

Namib Desert Horses are the only feral horses living in southern Africa. They manage to survive the heat of the Namib Desert, where temperatures can often soar to 113°F (45°C). Today, there are fewer than 300 of them left.

Tough conditions

Despite the harsh environment they live in, Namib Desert Horses keep in good condition, except when there is a severe drought. Young foals are hunted and killed by a variety of predators in the desert, including hyenas and jackals.

Mountain mules

Mules are the offspring of female horses and male donkeys. Strong and resilient, they are sure-footed on steep mountain trails and able to cope with extremes of hot and cold. These mules are carrying goods along the Annapurna Circuit, a tough 180-mile (300-km) trek around the Annapurna Mountains in Nepal. Pictured here is the route's highest point, 18,000 ft (5,500 m) above sea level.

ALL IN THE FAMILY

Horses belong to a group of animals called the equids. Other close members of the family include donkeys, zebras, and wild asses. All equids can interbreed with one another, but their hybrid offspring are rarely able to breed themselves. However, hybrids can be hardier than either of their parents, and the mule is a good example of this as it has long been prized as a tough, reliable, and enduring work-animal.

Asian wild asses

Also called onagers, these hardy equines live in the high grasslands and cold deserts of Asia, stretching from Iran to Mongolia. They have shorter legs than most horses, but are still among the fastest of all mammals, and can run at speeds of up to 40 mph (64 km/h). This allows them to outpace their main natural enemies, wolves.

The Mongolian wild ass, or khulan

A herd of kiang on the Tibetan Plateau

Donkeys

Donkeys were domesticated 5,000 years ago from the African wild ass to work as "beasts of burden." Only a few hundred of their wild cousins survive, but there are an estimated 40 million donkeys worldwide. In many parts of the world, they are still put to work, carrying goods or pulling carts. They are small and tough, with an average height of about 10 hands at the withers. Donkeys have a reputation for stubbornness due to a strong instinct for self-preservation. They will often refuse to do a task that they think is dangerous.

Mother and foal of the African wild ass, an ancestor of the donkey

A braying donkey

Zebras

Unlike horses or asses, none of the three species of zebra has ever been domesticated. They live on the grasslands of Africa, where their distinctive stripes are thought to make it harder for predators to pick out individuals from herds. Like human fingerprints, each zebra has its own unique pattern of stripes.

A herd of plains zebras drinking at a water hole

The zonkey, a cross between a male zebra and a female donkey

Thoroughbred horses jumping
a fence in a steeplechase

HOTBLOODS

Despite their name, the blood of hotbloods is the same temperature as that of other horses. Their name actually tells us that they have fiery personalities and are more spirited than warm- and cold-blooded horses.

Hotbloods originate from hot, dry parts of the world such as Egypt. Built to survive in desert climates, they are short-haired and have slender bodies with powerful haunches and long legs. They were taken to Europe from the Middle East and North Africa when European breeders decided they wanted to use them as light cavalry horses because they were faster and more agile than the European breeds.

Hotbloods are purebred, meaning that these breeds are not crossbred with warmbloods or coldbloods. Highly strung, emotional, and temperamental, hotbloods can be hard to handle—after all, they come from desert regions and may not feel as comfortable elsewhere. But they are also among the fastest, most beautiful, and most sought-after horses in the world. Kept in a good conditions, and with an experienced owner, as well as the right trainer and rider, these people-oriented breeds can become world-famous. These are the horses that you see lined up at race tracks, and the fastest among them—the gold cup winners—are worth millions of dollars.

A black Arabian in pasture

ARABIAN

MIDDLE EASTERN HOTBLOOD

The Arabian horse is prized for its speed, stamina, beauty, and, like other hotbloods, its spirited nature. With an elegant body shape and fine, wedge-shaped face, the Arabian has been used to improve almost every other horse breed in the world. It is one of the oldest breeds and can be traced back to 2500 BCE, to the deserts of the Middle East and to the nomadic people living there, today known as the Bedouin.

Ancient breed
This ancient Roman mosaic, dating from the 1st century CE, depicts a horse with similar characteristics to the Arabian breed in a hunting scene. Images of Arabian-type horses are found in artworks from several civilizations of the ancient world, including Mesopotamia, ancient Egypt, and many parts of the Roman empire.

Breed name: Arabian

Other name: Arab horse

Breed purpose: breeding, racing, riding, showing

Size: 15 hands

Coat color: chestnut, gray, bay, and black

Place of origin: Middle East

Ancestors: unknown

The **blood** of **Arabians** flows in **all breeds** of light horses.

War horse
The Arabian horse Marengo was a favorite of the French emperor Napoleon Bonaparte. A fan of gray Arabian horses, Napoleon kept 150 of them in his stud. Marengo was named after a famous French victory at the Battle of Marengo in 1800.

Desert dweller
Arabian horses first lived in the deserts of the Arabian peninsula, where there is very little water or grazing. As a result, they became almost totally reliant on humans for food and water, so it was crucial they developed an easy-going relationship with their owners and a good-natured temperament.

Worldwide favorite
The Arabian's finely chiseled wedge-shaped face with its large nostrils and expressive eyes have made this beautiful horse a favorite around the world. Different types of Arabians have their own devoted followers, some of whom value the horse most for its beauty and others for its stamina and athleticism. Although they are found around the world, the United States has the largest number of Arabians of any nation.

Special features
Many Arabians have a slight bulge located between their eyes. This is called the jibbah *by the Bedouin.*

Flying high
The Arabian has a distinctive tail, which is higher-set than many other breeds.

Something missing?
Some Arabians have one fewer lumbar vertebrae (small bones that form the backbone) than other breeds, which results in a shorter back.

Coat colors
Chestnut, bay, and gray are the most common colors for Arabians; black is less common. All Arabians have black skin, whatever their coat color.

Chestnut

Gray

Black

Muscular body
The horse's compact body provides a firm anchor point for its powerful muscles.

Powerful hindquarters
These are great for intensive events such as reining, where the rider guides a horse through a short pattern of turns, spins, and stops.

Floating movement
The Arabian in full flight is a wonder to see. The arched neck, high-set tail, and elegant body shape of this horse results in a very smooth-flowing gait (forward motion). The horse has such a light movement that is appears to be on springs, a trait that makes it perfect for equestrian sports.

ARABIAN BEAUTIES

FOUNDATION OF BREEDS WORLDWIDE

The Arabian has been used to improve almost every known horse breed around the world, adding elegance, speed, stamina, and intelligence. Modern Arabian breeds are sometimes called after their founding stallions, such as the Gidran Arab, which was named after Siglavy Gidran, a magnificent stallion born in Syria in 1810 and famed for his superb offspring.

ANGLO-ARAB

ENGLAND AND FRANCE

France is one of the great breeders of the Anglo-Arab, a cross between the Thoroughbred (*see pp.44–45*) and the Arabian (*see pp.32–33*). From its origins in England, the breed was perfected at Pompadour in Limousin, the national stud of France once favored by French rulers.

Breed name: Anglo-Arab	
Other name: Anglo-Arabian	
Breed purpose: riding	
Size: 15.2–16.3 hands	
Coat color: all solid colors	
Places of origin: England and France	
Ancestors: Arabian, Thoroughbred	

Supreme sports horse
Anglo-Arabs are strong and athletic, allowing them to perform quick bursts of acceleration and rapid changes of direction. This makes them perfect for equestrian sports such as show-jumping and cross-country.

Taking a jump at a cross-country event

Competing at show jumping

Smooth touch
The mane, coat, and tail are fine and sillky.

Solid frame
Today the Anglo-Arab is similar in appearance to the Thoroughbred, but it has a more solid frame and is generally taller than the average Arabian.

Tall Arab
Thanks to the introduction of some non-Arab breeding lines, the Shagya Arab is a little taller and bigger boned than purebred Arabians. But it retains the main Arab qualities, such as a high-set tail and wedge-shaped face.

SHAGYA ARAB

HUNGARY

The Shagya Arab was originally bred in the 19th century in Báblona as a riding horse for the Hungarian cavalry. The breed was founded on the cream-colored Arab stallion, Shagya, born in Syria in 1830. This is a fast and hardy horse, well-suited to sporting events such as dressage and eventing.

Breed name: Shagya Arab	**Coat color:** mainly gray, but also bay, chestnut, and black
Other name: Shagya Arabian	
Breed purpose: riding	**Place of origin:** Hungary
Breed size: 15 hands	**Ancestors:** Arabian, Thoroughbred, Spanish

SARDINIAN ANGLO-ARAB

SARDINIA, ITALY

These horses were first bred on the Mediterranean island of Sardinia. Arabians were imported in 1908 and Thoroughbreds in the 1920s to improve the tough island breed. Sardinian Anglo-Arabs are now used for various sporting events.

Breed name: Sardinian Anglo-Arab
Other name: Sardinian
Breed purpose: riding
Size: 15.2 hands
Coat color: chestnut, brown, bay, gray, black
Place of origin: Sardinia, Italy
Ancestors: Arabian

Built for speed
This breed has great speed and stamina, and sturdy legs suited to racing. Many take part in the Palio de Siena, a famous race where teams from different parts of Siena, Italy, race around the city's streets.

POLISH ARAB

POLAND

Pure Arabians have been bred in Poland since the 16th century. World War I and World War II saw the breed almost decimated, with huge numbers killed in battle or taken to Russia. However, breeders evacuated some of the horses and this helped to save the breed.

Breed name: Polish Arab
Other name: n/a
Breed purpose: riding, racing
Size: 14–15 hands
Coat color: bay, black, chestnut, or gray
Place of origin: Poland
Ancestors: Arabian

Prized racehorse
After the wars, the Polish Arabs, which were mainly bred for the racetrack, became particularly renowned for their quality. Today, Polish-bred Arabians are still used for racing and breeding and are traded around the world.

RUSSIAN ARAB

RUSSIA

There were Arabian horses in Russia as long ago as the 12th century, and it is thought that the first tsar, Ivan the Terrible (1530–84), kept Arabians in the royal stables. In 1889, a Russian nobleman called Count Stroganov set up the stud "Tersk," which later became a state-controlled breeding farm.

Breed name: Russian Arab
Other name: n/a
Breed purpose: riding
Size: 15.3–17 hands
Coat color: various
Place of origin: Russia
Ancestors: Arabian

Robust and powerful
A muscular and powerful horse with good speed and agility, the Gidran Arab is well suited to competitive sports and excels at jumping. The larger animals make good carriage horses.

GIDRAN ARAB

HUNGARY

This rare breed was created at Hungary's oldest national stud, Mezöhegyes, which was established in 1784 to breed military horses. It can be traced back to the chestnut Arabian stallion Siglavy Gidran, which was bought in Egypt by Baron Fechtig in 1816. The stallion's son was taken to Mezöhegyes, and the Gidran Arab was developed.

Breed name: Gidran Arab
Other name: n/a
Breed purpose: for the military, carriage work
Size: 16–17 hands
Coat color: mainly chestnut
Place of origin: Hungary
Ancestors: Arabian, Thoroughbred

The "sport of kings"

Most horse races last about two minutes, but for many people those two minutes are the most exciting time they can have. Here, horses thunder round a bend in the Greyville Racecourse, Durban, South Africa, in 2015. Horses that take part in flat races like this one are bred for their strength, speed, and athleticism. The horse that is most well-known among these racers is the Thoroughbred (*see pp.44–45*), but the Arabian *(see pp.32–33)*, Quarter Horse (*see pp.50–51*), and Appaloosa (*see pp.68–69*), excel on the flat as well.

BARB

HARDY NORTH AFRICAN HOTBLOOD

The Barb is a tough desert horse that probably first roamed wild in North Africa. It is named after the Berber people who brought the Barb to Europe when they invaded Spain in the 8th century. Like the Arabian, the Barb is fast, with great stamina and endurance, but its build is generally heavier and stockier than the Arabian, and it has a lower-placed tail.

Breed name: Barb

Other name: Berber horse

Breed purpose: breeding, riding, equestrian games

Size: 14.2–15.2 hands

Coat color: black, brown, bay, and gray

Place of origin: North Africa

Ancestors: possibly Arabian, Akhal Teke, Caspian

Face
The head tapers to a small muzzle, the forehead is broad, and the eyes are expressive.

Neck and back
The slightly arched neck leads to a relatively short, but strong, back.

Hindquarters
The tail is set low on hindquarters that are sloping and narrow.

Eager to learn
The Barb has a willing personality, is eager to learn, and can be trained for a variety of purposes. As they were once desert horses, they are hardy animals with real stamina. They are able to travel long distances with limited food and water supplies.

Front
The front of the body is powerful with high withers.

Sprinter
Powerful leg muscles allow the Barb to take off quickly and gallop like a sprinter.

Berber armies
North African Berbers rode desert horses, the ancestors of the Barb horse. Often used for close-combat fighting, Berber armies valued these tough horses for their speed and stamina. Now the Barb is bred primarily in Morocco, Algeria, southern France, and Spain, although the number of Barbs in North Africa is declining.

Coat colors

The most common Barb color is gray, but they can also be found in all solid colors, including buckskin, dun, and roan.

Black

Brown

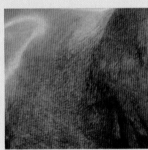

Bay

Spanish Barb

A variety known as the Spanish Barb is bred in the United States. Extensive cross-breeding and slaughter almost led to the end of the Spanish Barb in the late 19th century, but ranchers managed to save the breed.

Prized by nobility

King Richard II of England (right) is said to have owned a Barb horse in the 14th century, and two centuries later, King Henry VIII bought the horses for his stables. In fact, Barbs were highly prized by nobility right across Europe from Spain to Italy.

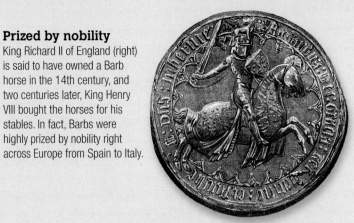

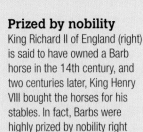

The Barb is second only **to the Arabian** in the development of **breeds** worldwide.

The Andalusian, descendant of the Barb

Worldwide influence

The Barb has played a major role in the development of breeds around the world. Mixed with Spanish horses, it became the magnificent Andalusian (*see pp.96–97*), and it was used to develop the Thoroughbred (*see pp.44–45*) as well as many other breeds, including the Mustang (*see pp.22–23*).

Barb with an Arabian face

Terracotta horses

There is ample archaeological evidence of the importance of horses in ancient China. These sculpted horses are part of the Terracotta Army, an extraordinary buried collection of life-size sculptures first discovered in China in 1974 by farmers digging a water well. The sculptures are of men, equipment, and horses of the Chinese emperor Qin Shi Huang, who died in 210 BCE. So far, archeologists have uncovered 8,000 soldiers and 670 horses, as well as many other items, including chariots.

THE ANCIENT WORLD

In the ancient world, people around the world learned how to control horses for the first time. The animals played a central role in everyday life, assuming a wide range of roles in farming, transportation, sport, and warfare. The success or failure of military campaigns often depended on the quality of an army's horses. A good horse was a prized possession, and paintings and statues were created to celebrate them.

Medieval horseshoe

Honored warhorses

The ancient Greeks prized their horses so highly that there are stories of the animals being given wheat and wine instead of barley and water. They were also thought to be too important to use in warfare. Until the arrival of the Macedonian general Alexander the Great (356–323 BCE), their military roles were limited to scouting and pulling wagons. Alexander's warhorse was called Bucephalus and he valued the animal so much that, when it was killed in battle, he founded a city named Bucephala in its honor.

Alexander the Great riding into battle on Bucephalus

Protecting the hooves

As people put horses to work, they soon discovered that the hooves needed extra protection. The Romans secured pieces of metal to the hooves using leather straps, but these could slip off. Shoes secured by nails first appeared in the 10th century CE, and nailed-on horseshoes soon became widespread. Early horseshoes were cast in bronze, which was replaced with harder-wearing iron by the 13th and 14th centuries.

Horse-drawn chariots

In the ancient world, the chariot was the supreme military weapon, as well as being used for hunting and sporting competitions. Usually on two wheels and drawn by two horses, it carried a driver and a fighter. In ancient Rome, brutal chariot races were held in front of huge crowds, four teams with three chariots each racing each other.

The British Iceni warrior queen Boudicca on her scythed chariot

On the steppes

From the 9th century BCE onward, ancient texts talk of nomadic tribes known as Scythians who lived in the central Eurasian steppes. These herders would spend almost the entire day on horseback, moving across the grasslands with their cattle and sheep. They were among the first to master the art of mounted warfare, and settled farmers living in towns and cities came to fear raids by the Scythian archers.

A modern reenactment of mounted Scythian archery

A female Scythian mounted archer

AKHAL-TEKE
CENTRAL ASIAN HOTBLOOD

The Akhal-Teke is one of the oldest horse breeds in the world. A rare horse from the deserts of Turkmenistan, it probably dates back some 3,000 years to the now-extinct Turkoman horse. The Akhal-Teke was prized by local tribespeople who used them to raid settlements on the harsh steppes of central Asia. Many Akhal-Tekes have a metallic sheen to their coat, and the breed has a reputation for its speed and stamina.

Breed name: Akhal-Teke

Other names: n/a

Breed purpose: raiding and racing

Size: 15–16 hands

Coat color: mostly bay and dun, black, chestnut, palomino, gray

Place of origin: Turkmenistan

Ancestors: Turkoman, Thoroughbred

Spirited and agile
Akhal-Teke horses are named after the Teke Turkmen tribe that lived around the Akhal oasis in Turkmenistan. Having been bred for raiding in a tough environment, they are a hardy and resilient breed that are well known for their endurance. They are also fast and agile, and have a spirited temperament.

In 1935, **Akhal-Teke horses** were ridden across **a desert** for more than **three** days **without water**.

Sporting stars
Akhal-Teke horses are bred all around the world, although all of them now have the Thoroughbred (*see pp.44–45*) as part of their ancestry. Today, the breed excels in sport, particularly in track racing, dressage, show jumping, and cross-country endurance racing.

Refined head
Small, refined head with long ears and "hooded" or almond-shaped eyes.

National emblem
Akhal-Teke horses appear on the banknotes and coat of arms in Turkmenistan, as well as on postage stamps of Turkmenistan, Russia, Azerbaijan, and Kazakhstan. A large number of monuments in Turkmenistan are also dedicated to the breed.

Legs and hooves
The straight forelegs end in small but hardy hooves.

Coat colors
Akhal-Tekes are well known for their golden palomino or buckskin coats. However, their most common colors are bay, dun, chestnut, black, and gray.

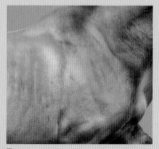
Dun

Bay

Chestnut

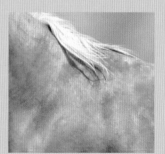
Palomino

Beautiful desert racer
The Akhal-Teke has a graceful, athletic appearance, with a long, strong back and narrow head. Its look has often been compared to that of a cheetah or greyhound. The skin of an Akhal-Teke is thin, while its coat and hair are fine. Many Akhal-Teke horses have exceptionally shiny coats, which add to their beauty.

THOROUGHBRED

ENGLISH HOTBLOOD

As the world's most talented racing horse, the hotblooded Thoroughbred is celebrated for its exceptional athleticism and spirited character. All Thoroughbreds have ancestry that can be traced back to three foundation stallions that were taken to England from the Middle East in the late 17th and early 18th centuries. Today, Thoroughbreds are the fastest, most commercially valuable breed in the world.

Flexible tail
This is used to help with balance while racing.

Breed name: Thoroughbred

Other names: English Thoroughbred

Breed purpose: flat racing and many equestrian sports

Size: 15.2–17 hands

Coat color: brown, bay, chestnut, black, and gray

Place of origin: England

Ancestors: Arab, Barb, Turkomen, native "running horses"

The **fastest** recorded **Thoroughbred** horse was **Winning Brew** in 2008, **sprinting** at **43.97 mph** (70.76 km/h) at Penn National racecourse in **Pennsylvania**.

Powerhouse
Powerful haunches carry the weight and have great flexibility.

Super studs

All Thoroughbred horses can be traced back to one or more of three foundation stallions: the Byerley Turk (imported 1689), the Darley Arabian (imported 1704), and the Godolphin Arabian (imported 1728). A recent scientific study found that a staggering 95 percent of the 500,000 Thoroughbreds alive today are descended from the Darley Arabian (above).

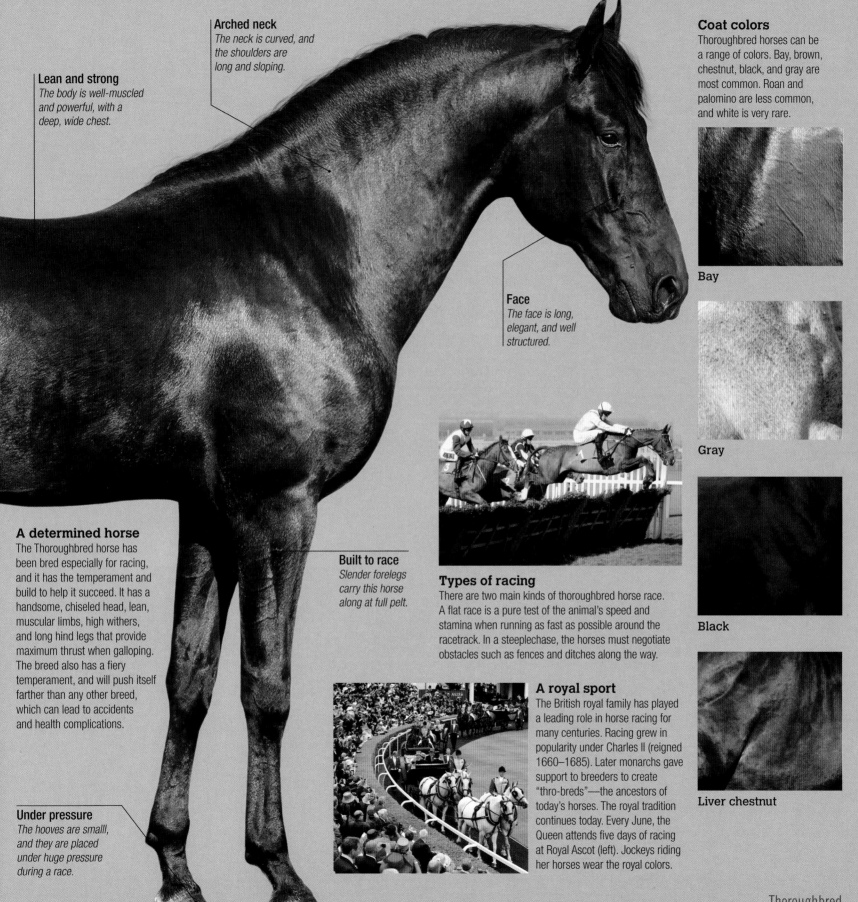

Arched neck
The neck is curved, and the shoulders are long and sloping.

Lean and strong
The body is well-muscled and powerful, with a deep, wide chest.

Coat colors
Thoroughbred horses can be a range of colors. Bay, brown, chestnut, black, and gray are most common. Roan and palomino are less common, and white is very rare.

Bay

Gray

Black

Liver chestnut

Face
The face is long, elegant, and well structured.

A determined horse
The Thoroughbred horse has been bred especially for racing, and it has the temperament and build to help it succeed. It has a handsome, chiseled head, lean, muscular limbs, high withers, and long hind legs that provide maximum thrust when galloping. The breed also has a fiery temperament, and will push itself farther than any other breed, which can lead to accidents and health complications.

Built to race
Slender forelegs carry this horse along at full pelt.

Types of racing
There are two main kinds of thoroughbred horse race. A flat race is a pure test of the animal's speed and stamina when running as fast as possible around the racetrack. In a steeplechase, the horses must negotiate obstacles such as fences and ditches along the way.

A royal sport
The British royal family has played a leading role in horse racing for many centuries. Racing grew in popularity under Charles II (reigned 1660–1685). Later monarchs gave support to breeders to create "thro-breds"—the ancestors of today's horses. The royal tradition continues today. Every June, the Queen attends five days of racing at Royal Ascot (left). Jockeys riding her horses wear the royal colors.

Under pressure
The hooves are smalll, and they are placed under huge pressure during a race.

LUSITANO

SPAIN AND PORTUGAL

This horse is closely related to the Spanish Andalusian horse (*see pp.96–97*). In 1966, the breed was officially named Lusitano after the ancient Roman province Lusitania, which included most of modern-day Portugal. The horse has been bred independently in Portugal for more than 200 years. Lusitanos make excellent dressage horses and they have competed in several Olympics as well as in international show jumping and combined-driving events.

Palace guards
Portugal's National Republican Guard ride Lusitano horses while on duty in front of the presidential palace in Lisbon. Once a month, the changing of the guard provides a great spectacle as the horses march and gallop in time.

Breed name: Lusitano

Other name: Pure Blood Lusitano

Breed purpose: agriculture, war, riding

Size: 15.1–16.1 hands

Coat color: usually gray, or all solid colors

Place of origin: Spain and Portugal

Ancestors: Iberian, Barb

Fast learner
An agile and strong horse, the Lusitano is also very easily trained. This is why it has proved so successful on the parade ground and in the show ring. On the move, it is finely balanced and has a powerful high leg action.

Handsome features
The head is slim and well-proportioned, with a slightly convex profile.

Angled behind
The hindquarters are rounded and sloped which gives the breed a low-set tail.

Riding power
Strong muscular legs lead up to a thick, broad chest.

Stage presence
Nicknamed the "Flying Frenchman," horse trainer Lorenzo performs a show with a troop of 12 Lusitanos. His many daring stunts include standing on the backs of two horses.

Good-natured

Pintabians are graceful, lively horses that are prized for their beauty, stamina, and friendly nature, which makes them a popular breed. They have wide-set eyes, a short and strong back, and a high-set tail.

PINTABIAN

UNITED STATES

This are a very new and popular breed, first created in the 1990s. It is mostly of Arabian blood, but has white patches on its coat, which are not found in purebred Arabians. The name Pintabian merges "pinto" (a coat pattern made of patches of white) and "Arabian."

Breed name: Pintabian	Size: 14.2–15.2 hands
Other name: n/a	Coat color: tobiano (white patches)
Breed purpose: general riding, dressage, endurance racing, show horse	Place of origin: US
	Ancestors: Arabian

TERSK

NORTHERN CAUCASUS, RUSSIA

The Tersk was bred in Russia from the 1920s. The aim was to replace the almost-extinct Strelets Arabian breed. Two Strelets stallions and a few mares were sent to the Russian state stud of Tersk and bred with three Arabian stallions and some crossbreed mares. This created a beautiful, bold, and fast new breed.

Breed name: Tersk
Other name: n/a
Breed purpose: breeding, racing, sporting events
Size: 15 hands
Coat color: gray
Place of origin: northern Caucasus, Russia
Ancestors: Strelets Arabian, purebred Arabian, Gidran

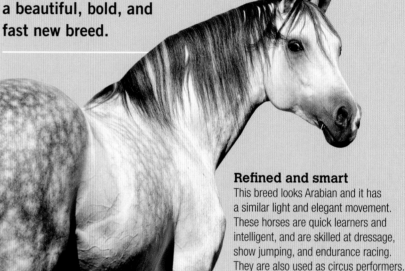

Refined and smart

This breed looks Arabian and it has a similar light and elegant movement. These horses are quick learners and intelligent, and are skilled at dressage, show jumping, and endurance racing. They are also used as circus performers.

Breed name: Maremmano
Other name: n/a
Breed purpose: livestock herding
Size: 15.3 hands
Coat color: any solid color
Place of origin: Italy
Ancestors: Arab, Barb, Thoroughbred, Norfolk Roadster

Working horse

With a strong build, sturdy legs, and good stamina, this breed is well suited to herding cattle. It is not a fast horse, but it is good-natured and calm.

MAREMMANO

ITALY

The Maremmano is a robust breed that was originally developed for herding cattle in the Maremma coastal region of Tuscany and Lazio. It also proved to be a reliable troop horse and was involved in one of the last cavalry charges in World War II, carrying Italian cavalry into battle against Russian soldiers in 1942. Today, the Maremmano is used by the Italian Mounted Police and by the last few remaining *butteri*, cowboys who work cattle in the Maremma Regional Park in Tuscany.

The Canadian mounties ride black horses with Thoroughbred and Hanoverian bloodlines.

WARMBLOODS

These middle-weight horses were originally bred for riding or pulling carriages. The largest group of light horses, warmbloods fall somewhere between the hotblood racing horses and coldblood draft horses.

Warmbloods are far more laid back than the highly strung hotbloods, but still have great sporting ability, albeit at different sports. They are the top choice for show jumping, dressage, and eventing—sports that require both athleticism and a cool head. Warmblood studs put an emphasis on performance rather than pure breeding, which means that cross-breeding is usually allowed by the stud registries to improve particular breeds. Many of these horses are bred to be outstanding at a particular sport, while others are developed to be easy to handle by all types of leisure rider, with or without a saddle.

These breeds produce some of the best riding horses for all levels of ability. Many breeds are great for trekking and endurance, while others are excellent for children or inexperienced riders. That does not mean that warmbloods have not been used for work. The heavier breeds did farm work in the past, and many were and are splendid carriage horses. Their calm temperament makes several breeds suitable for police horses today.

Taking a jump at a cross-country event in Moscow, Russia

AMERICAN QUARTER HORSE

WARMBLOOD OF THE AMERICAN FRONTIER

The American Quarter Horse was the favorite mount for cowboys of the old American West. It is compact, hardy, and lightning-quick, and was originally bred to herd cows and to race short distances. Today, there are around 3 million American Quarter Horses registered around the world and it is still the most popular horse breed in the US. These horses can still be found working on ranches, as well as competing in rodeos, horse shows, and racing events.

New breed
The breed began in Virginia and the Carolinas where settlers bred their horses with Chickasaw Native American mares. Later, Thoroughbred bloodlines were introduced. By the late 17th century, the horses were being raced successfully over quarter-mile (0.4 km) courses, and these races are the origin of the breed's name.

Breed name: American Quarter Horse

Other name: Quarter Horse

Breed purpose: farm work, pleasure riding, racing, shows, and competitions

Breed size: 14.3–16 hands

Coat color: all colors, most commonly chestnut

Place of origin: Virginia, US

Ancestors: Barb, Arabian, Thoroughbred, Mustang

Quarter Horses can race at speeds of up to 55 miles (88 km) an hour.

Hardworking and tough
During the 19th century, settlers pushed westward across the North American continent. In the new frontier states of the American West, the hard-working and agile American Quarter Horses proved popular as they had a real instinct for working with cattle and could almost second-guess the needs of their riders.

Rodeo ride
The majority of the horses that take part in rodeo events are American Quarter Horses. They are an ideal size for most events as they are fast over short distances and small enough to make sharp turns inside the arena. Rodeo events include bareback and saddle bronc riding (left), in which a cowboy must stay on top of a bucking horse for at least eight seconds.

Stock and racing

American Quarter Horses are sure-footed and agile, and they are excellent sprinters over short distances. They generally have a calm nature and are easy to train, making them good horses for beginners or families. There are two main body types of American Quarter Horse: the hunter or racing type, used primarily for racing, and the stock type, used mainly for ranching.

Fine features
The finely chiseled head shows the horse's Thoroughbred heritage.

Fast turner
Powerful and broad hindquarters give the American Quarter Horse plenty of power and enable it to turn quickly, with agility and speed.

Tail carriage
The horse has rounded hindquarters, which means that the tail sits a little lower than many other breeds.

Long-legged sprinter
Racing Quarter Horses have longer legs and they are leaner than the stock horse.

Coat colors

The most common color for the American Quarter Horse is chestnut. While spotted color patterns, such as flea bitten, were originally excluded, they are now accepted as long as both parents have had their DNA registered.

Dapple gray

Chestnut

Dun

Fast-paced teamwork

The game of polo is the oldest of the equestrian sports. A version was played in central Asia by mounted nomads as long ago as 600 BCE, as a training game for cavalry with as many as 100 men a side. In time, polo became a sport played by two teams of four players carrying mallets whose aim is to drive a wooden ball between two goal posts. Polo was introduced to India in the 13th century, and here, it is being played at the oldest existing polo club in the world, the Calcutta Polo Club (CPC), established in 1862 in Kolkata in West Bengal.

Southern beauty

The Tennessee Walking Horse is a popular show breed that has a range of striking coat colors and patterns. It is found throughout the United States, but is most common in the southern states, where many horse shows dedicate special events to this breed to showcase its unique riding qualities. The breed's docile nature makes it a first choice for trekkers, and very suitable for nervous riders.

TENNESSEE WALKING HORSE

HIGH-STEPPING WARMBLOOD

The Tennessee Walking Horse is famed for its unique way of moving. It has a naturally flowing riding gait and is best known for its style of running-walk. The breed was developed in the mid-19th century to work on the farms and plantations of Tennessee and was originally known as a "turn-row" as it could quickly move around crop rows in plantations. With a calm temperament and smooth movement, it has since become a popular riding horse.

Breed name: Tennessee Walking Horse

Other names: Tennessee Walker, Walker, Turn Row, Plantation Walking Horse

Breed purpose: general riding, horse shows, dressage, jumping, eventing, farm work

Size: 14.3–17 hands

Coat color: any solid color and several patterned colors

Place of origin: Tennessee, US

Ancestors: Thoroughbred, American Standardbred, Narrangansett Pacer, Morgan, Saddlebred, Mustang

Fine face
The head is well-defined and elegant, with small ears.

Tall and handsome
This tall horse can stand 17 hands at the withers, and its long neck gives it an impressive presence. These striking features have made it a regular on TV, and given it many famous admirers. Rock star Elvis Presley kept a number of Tennessee Walking Horses at his home, Graceland, including his favorite horse, Bear.

Coat colors
Tennessee Walkers can be found in any solid color as well as several patterned colors, including overo, sabino, and tobiano.

Buckskin

Pinto

Palomino

Hindquarters
The back is short and hindquarters moderately muscled.

Underside
The bottom line of the horse is longer than the top line to allow for a long stride.

High stepper
The Tennessee Walking Horse is well-known for its famous running-walk. This is performed with a quick, high-stepping movement, where each foot hits the ground separately. The horse also nods its head and neck up and down in rhythm with each step.

Flowing motion
The Tennessee Walking Horse uses long, brisk strides when walking. To move faster, it adopts a type of smooth running-walk that is described as "bounce free." When the Tennessee Walking Horse canters, the action is so comfortable that riders describe it as a smooth "rocking chair" motion.

KNOW THE GAIT

The term "gait" refers to the sequence in which a horse puts its hooves down, known as a footfall pattern. Most horses have four natural gaits—walk, trot, canter, and gallop—which are all distinct and recognizable. There are additional gaits that are less common, or need to be trained, such as "ambling gaits." Breeds that can move with an ambling gait are often referred to as "gaited horses," particularly in the US, where they are most common.

WALK

IN NO HURRY

A horse's walk has a clear, four-beat rhythm. As the animal moves along, its rib cage sways from side to side as its weight shifts. The pace is regular and predictable, and each step is felt by the rider. The footfall pattern is simple: 1) left hind; 2) left fore; 3) right hind; 4) right fore. This is the first gait for a new rider to learn.

Saving energy
Grazing horses move around their pasture with a gentle, unhurried walk. This is the easiest way for a horse to get around while expending the least amount of energy.

Extended trot
In dressage competitions, a horse is expected to perform a number of controlled moves. One of the hardest to master is the extended trot, in which the horse moves in a trotting gait while lengthening its stride as much as possible.

TROT

BREAKING INTO A TROT

Slightly faster than a walk, the trot follows a two-beat rhythm, with a springy feel. The horse puts down one diagonal pair of feet, followed swiftly by the opposite pair. The footfall pattern is: 1) right fore and left hind; 2) all feet raised; 3) left fore and right hind.

CANTER

PICKING UP THE PACE

A horse's canter is faster than its trot. It looks like a rocking movement, forward and backward, as the horse's weight shifts from front to back. It has a three-beat rhythm and is one of the two fastest gaits. The footfall pattern is: 1) left hind; 2) left fore and right hind together; 3) right fore.

Different styles

Each breed of horse has a slightly different style of canter. The Friesian has a powerful movement with a high leg action. Despite this, a well-trained Friesian gives a comfortable ride, making the rider feel that they are on a gentle rocking horse.

GALLOP

MOVING AT FULL PELT

This is the fastest gait and usually follows a four-beat rhythm. Like the canter, the movement is rocking, but the rhythm may vary depending on the speed. A horse's gallop can be very fast—the average speed is 25–30 mph (40–48 kph). The footfall pattern is normally: 1) left hind; 2) right hind; 3) left fore; 4) right fore.

Stampede

A herd of Arabian horses in full gallop is an awesome sight. Herds of horses may break into a gallop in an uncontrolled stampede if they feel under threat.

AMBLE

OTHER RARE OR TRAINED GAITS

There are various less common gaits that are faster than a walk and slower than a canter, often called "ambling gaits." Unlike standard gaits, the horse moves its legs in lateral (side by side) rather than diagonal pairs—both left legs work as a pair, and both right legs work as a pair. Ambling gaits are associated with US breeds, and have been refined in the US, but the style is found in Asia and Europe too.

Inherited moves

The ambling gait is passed down from parents to their foals and only occurs naturally in some breeds. The Indian Kathiawari, North American Standardbred, and South America Peruvian Paso (right) are all "gaited horses."

Hard work on horseback

Argentinian "*gauchos*" (cowboys) round up their sheep in Los Glaciares National Park in Patagonia. In remote areas such as this, ranchers often spend long hours in the saddle. These skilled horsemen use a wide saddle similar to the western saddle of their North American counterparts. The rider sits on a layer of sheepskin for added comfort during a long working day.

TACKING UP

Before you can mount your horse, you need to tack up. The tack includes equipment such as the saddle, bridle, reins, harnesses, and the bit. Different styles of tack are needed depending on how the horse will be ridden. For example, in a short race, a small saddle is used, while for long rides, wider saddles are better as they reduce the pressure on a horse's back. Tacking up must be done properly to ensure the safety and comfort of both horse and rider.

Stirrups
The stirrups provide the rider with a secure foot support, and allow them to raise up from the saddle to make faster riding more comfortable. On an English saddle, the stirrups are designed to come off the saddle in the event of an accident. The stirrups on a western saddle are fixed, but they are wider to stop the foot becoming trapped.

English stirrup

Western stirrup

Western saddle
This is the "cowboy" saddle familiar from the movies. The western saddle was developed by cattle ranchers in Mexico and is still widely used for working horses across the United States. At the front of the saddle is a horn, which was added to help tie up cattle. The saddle is designed to be used for many hours and is wider to make the ride more comfortable and reduce strain on the horse.

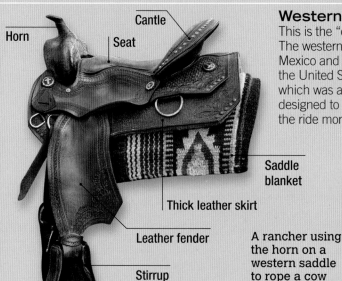

Horn

Cantle

Seat

Saddle blanket

Thick leather skirt

Leather fender

Stirrup

A rancher using the horn on a western saddle to rope a cow

Controlling with the bit
The bit is a metal bar placed in a horse's mouth. It rests on the gums between the front incisor teeth and the molars at the back, and is held in place by a bridle that is attached on either side to the reins. The rider communicates with the horse through the bit by tightening or loosening the grip on the reins. This must be done carefully, as incorrect use of the reins can hurt the horse.

Bit

English saddle
In most horse-riding competitions, the English saddle must be used. Smaller and lighter than the western saddle, it is designed to allow the horse maximum freedom of movement when running or jumping. This style of saddle offers closer contact with the horse's back than a western saddle.

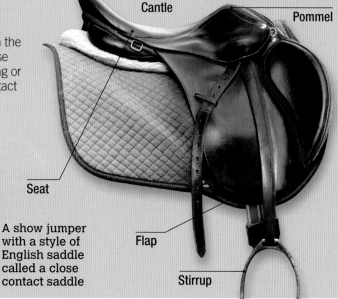

Cantle

Pommel

Seat

Flap

Stirrup

A show jumper with a style of English saddle called a close contact saddle

Horse with bit in place

MORGAN

ALL-ROUND PERFORMER

Today, Morgans are found in more than 20 countries around the world, but all of them can be traced back to one famous stallion named Figure. Born in Massachusetts in 1789, Figure was bought by the teacher Justin Morgan, who gave his name to the breed. No one knows for sure about Figure's ancestry, but he was well known as a strong and fast horse. The stallion produced three sons, Sherman, Woodbury, and Bulrush. Together, they established the first documented breed in North America that soon became famous for its beauty and strength.

Breed name: Morgan

Other names: n/a

Breed purpose: ranch work, racing

Size: 14.1–15.2 hands

Coat color: chestnut, bay, black, brown, palomino

Place of origin: Vermont, US

Ancestors: unknown

Striking features
The Morgan has a broad forehead and large, expressive eyes.

Public performer

At first, Morgans were used in a wide range of roles, including pulling a plow, driving a carriage, and carrying the owner to work. They also earned a reputation as good military horses. One of the best-known early Morgans was Hale's Green Mountain (above), born in 1832. He became famous for his crowd-pleasing performances at parades and military fairs.

Powerful mover
Strong legs help to give the horse its lively, fluid gait.

Popular choice

The Morgan horse has a strong and proud way of moving and its well-defined lines and attractive appearance have helped to make this breed popular globally. There are now thought to be more than 175,000 Morgan horses around the world. The breed is also intelligent, with an easy-going and calm temperament, making it an ideal general riding horse for both adults and children.

Sheridan's steed

During the Civil War, Union General Philip Sheridan famously rode a Morgan horse from Winchester, Virginia, to Cedar Creek, Virginia, on October 19, 1864. There he rallied his troops and turned almost certain defeat into victory at the Battle of Cedar Creek. Sheridan's horse lived to be almost 20 years old.

Coat colors

Morgans come in a variety of colors, including palomino (*see main image*), although bay, black, and brown are the colors most commonly seen.

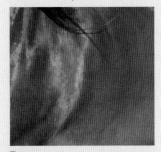

Bay

Black

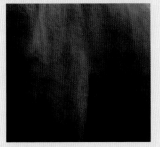

Liver chestnut

Strong back

The back is short and compact, while the hindquarters are packed with powerful muscles.

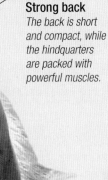

State symbol

The Morgan is one of the emblems for the state of Vermont in New England. The horse was first bred in Vermont and it has remained popular there to this day. The state still produces and protects the Morgan breed at the University of Vermont's Morgan Horse Farm at Weybridge.

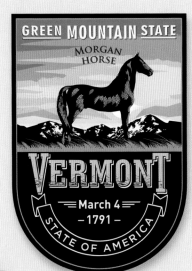

GREEN MOUNTAIN STATE

MORGAN HORSE

VERMONT

═ March 4 ═
─ 1791 ─

STATE OF AMERICA

Sporting star

Obedient, easy-to-train, and with a naturally strong movement, Morgan horses perform well in carriage driving and make good harness horses. They also do well at shows, excelling in a variety of events, including show jumping and dressage (left).

In **1972**, Disney made the movie ***Justin Morgan Had a Horse***, re-telling the story of how the Morgan **breed** was created.

The horses of war

During the American Civil War (1861–1865), horses performed vital tasks for both the Union and Confederate sides. This picture of a Union field artillery unit shows mounted senior officers supervising cannon being pulled into position by teams of six horses each, the men marching alongside. This first "modern" war used draft and packhorses as well as mules—around one million on the Union side alone—and there were many casualties. The Confederate general J. O. Shelby had 24 horses shot from under him, while General George A. Custer holds the Union record with the loss of 11 horses.

AMERICAN STANDARDBRED

FAST-TROTTING WARMBLOOD

The American Standardbred is the fastest trotting and pacing horse in the world, and a common sight on the racetracks of the United States in harness racing. Solid and strong, the breed can be traced back to a Thoroughbred stallion named Messenger, an English flat racing horse that was taken to the United States in 1788. Messenger's great-grandson, Hambletonian 10, sired horses that had exceptional trotting speed.

Breed name: American Standardbred

Other names: Rysdyk Standardbred

Breed purpose: trotting and harness racing

Size: 14–16 hands

Coat color: mainly bay, brown, black, and chestnut

Place of origin: New England, US

Ancestors: Thoroughbred, Morgan, Canadian Pacer, Narragansett Pacer

Champion breeder
Bought by a stable hand called William Rysdyk in 1849, Hambletonian 10 soon became well-known as a champion trotter. Rysdyk put him out to stud from an early age, and he went on to sire around 1,330 foals before he died in 1876.

Fast-paced sulky racing

Slow and steady Amish buggy

Change of pace
Standardbreds can hold their own in any driving discipline. In harness racing, they pull a two-wheeled racing cart known as a *sulky*. But they are easily retrained to pull buggies for everyday driving.

Coat colors
Most Standardbreds are bay, chestnut, liver chestnut, gray, black, and other solid colors. They rarely have white markings.

Red bay

Brown

Gray

In 1993, **Cambest** became the **fastest** Standardbred ever when he paced a mile in just **1 minute 46.20 seconds**.

Fine features
A broad forehead leads down a straight profile.

Long nose
The horse has a Roman nose with large nostrils.

Curved neck
The neck is long compared to other breeds and arched.

Flat haunches
The haunches are slightly higher than the withers and flatter-sided.

Good learner
This horse has a calm and good-natured temperament that makes it easy to train and ideal for all except the beginning rider. It is great both for trail riding and for work as a ranch horse, and it is versatile enough to take part in sports such as dressage and eventing.

The name Standardbred comes from the "standard" trotting or pacing speed required by the breed registry. In 1879, every Standardbred had to be able to trot a mile (1.6 km) in less than two minutes and 30 seconds. The horse's body and build show its racing background, with a long, muscular body and powerful shoulders and hindquarters to help with its long strides.

AZTECA

MEXICO

This rare breed combines the beauty of the Andalusian and the speed of the American Quarter Horse. Crossed with Criollo mares, the Azteca was developed by Mexican horsemen (*charro*) who wanted an agile new breed of horse to work on their cattle farms and ranches.

Breed name: Azteca	**Coat color:** almost all sold colors, gray is common, plus roan and pinto
Other name: n/a	**Place of origin:** Mexico
Breed purpose: ranch work, trail riding, dressage, bullfighting	**Ancestors:** Andalusian, American Quarter Horse, Mexican Criollo
Size: 14.2–16 hands	

Mexican style

The Azteca is well-built, elegant, and intelligent, with large feet and dense bones that contribute to its athletic ability. The first official Azteca was a stallion named Casarejo, born in Mexico in 1972, and the breed was soon adopted as the national horse of Mexico.

Azteca with a *charro*-style saddle and bridle

A traditional Azteca display

Dazzling display

Azteca horses were developed by cowboys from Mexico and shine in Western riding competitions. They are increasingly seen in English dressage, as well as polo and bullfighting events. Azteca Horses are often displayed at festivals in the US.

AMERICAN INDIAN HORSE

UNITED STATES

The American Indian Horse has coats of virtually every color and variation. It is hardy and sure-footed, with a wild and intelligent nature. The registry for the breed was set up in the US in 1961 with the aim to protect the pedigree of the American Indian Horse. Today, it is a popular breed for horse shows and speed events.

Breed name: American Indian Horse	**Coat color:** any color, pinto and leopard patterns common
Other name: Cow Pony, Buffalo Horse	**Place of origin:** United States
Breed purpose: riding, sports	**Ancestors:** Spanish Barb, Arabian, Mustang, Appaloosa
Size: 13–16 hands	

Buffalo hunting on horseback

Hunting companion
American Indian Horses are the descendants of Spanish horses first brought to the Americas in the 16th century. Native American people later began to use these horses to hunt buffalo, which provided them with food, shelter, tools and clothing.

Chestnut American Indian Horse

AMERICAN WARMBLOOD

UNITED STATES

The American Warmblood was created primarily for traditional sport disciplines, such as show jumping, eventing, and dressage. This breed has the characteristics found in many quality warmblood breeds. It is friendly, with a calm temperament and good intuition. And it is easy to train, which makes it a suitable horse for competitive events. It is also a great choice for less experienced riders.

Bred for sports
American Warmbloods share physical similarities to Thoroughbred, European warmblood, and Arabian horses, from which they are descended. They are well-buit with muscular hindquarters, a short back,and strong sloping shoulders. These traits help them excel in riding sport events.

Breed name: American Warmblood	**Coat color:** all solid colors
Other name: n/a	**Place of origin:** US
Breed purpose: sporting disciplines	**Ancestors:** Thoroughbred, Arabian European warmbloods, local draft breeds
Size: 15–17 hands	

APPALOOSA

EYE-CATCHING SPOTTED BREED

Instantly recognizable for their colorful and spotted coat patterns, Appaloosa horses are one of the most popular breeds in the United States. They are sturdy and versatile, well-suited to ranch work and herding cattle. The spotted horse was first referred to by white settlers of the US as the "Palouse horse," after the Palouse River that runs through Washington, Oregon, and Idaho, a region once inhabited by the Nez Perce tribe. By the late 1800s, the name had changed to Appaloosa.

Breed name: Appaloosa

Other name: n/a

Breed purpose: ranching, competition

Breed size: 14.2–15.2 hands

Coat color: spotted—various patterns, any solid color

Place of origin: US

Ancestors: unknown

Toy horse
Today, Appaloosa's are still widely used for working with cattle, as well as Western competitions, racing, and other equestrian events. They remain a much-reproduced symbol of the American West, becoming the official state horse of Idaho in 1975.

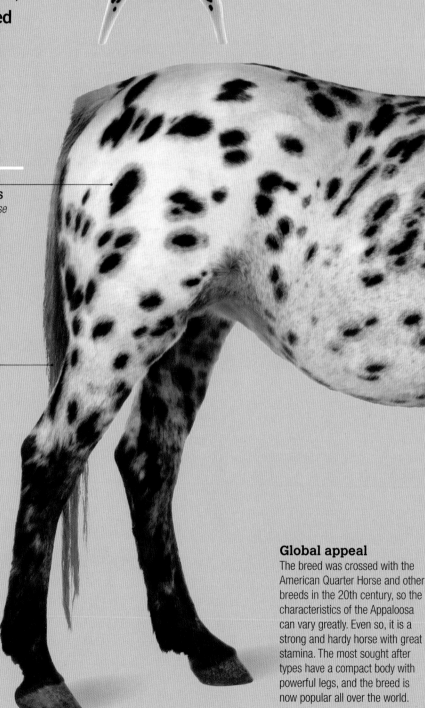

Changing spots
Over time, the base coat may change, and more spots may appear.

Thin tail
Like the mane, the tail of this horse is thin and sparse, and varies in length.

Tough survivor
The Appaloosa is linked with the Native American Nez Perce tribe of northwest America. These skilled horse breeders needed strong horses for war and hunting. When the US government seized Nez Perce land in the 1870s, only a few tough horses survived. The breed was revived from 1938 onward.

Global appeal
The breed was crossed with the American Quarter Horse and other breeds in the 20th century, so the characteristics of the Appaloosa can vary greatly. Even so, it is a strong and hardy horse with great stamina. The most sought after types have a compact body with powerful legs, and the breed is now popular all over the world.

Pointed ears
The ears are pointed, pricked, and medium-sized.

Bright eyes
The sclera, which encircles the iris of the eye, is white, not black.

Muzzle coloring
Spotting is less visible around the muzzle, and the skin is mottled.

Tufty mane
A wispy and short mane runs down the length of a long, slender neck.

White or striped?
If the legs have white markings, the hooves are white, and many Appaloosas have striped hooves.

The 1966 **Walt Disney** film **"Run, Appaloosa, Run"** is about a young **Nez Perce** girl who **raises** a **motherless** horse.

Coat patterns
Appaloosa horses have varying coat patterns, with spots that cover all or part of their bodies. Some horses have blanket patterns, which are large areas that are a single color.

Blanket

Leopard

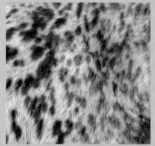
Marble

Snowflake

Prehistoric colors
Spotted horses have been represented in prehistoric art, and Chinese art dating back to 500 BCE. It is probable that Spanish settlers introduced "raindrop horses," ancestors of the Appaloosa, to the Americas in the 16th century.

Growing spots
Coat patterns develop in the course of a horse's life. Foals are born with coats that tend to darken once they have shed their baby hair. The blanket or leopard patterns are more likely to stay the same, but more visible spotting may appear as the horse gets older.

COLOR VARIATIONS

COAT COLORS AND PATTERNS

Amazingly, every horse is born with one of four base colors—chestnut, bay, brown, and black. There are many different variations to these colors and how they are mixed, which is why horses have different colors and markings. Black may have white hairs scattered over the body, and "brindle"—the presence of subtle zebra-like stripes—is very rare. Some coat colors look similar, like bay and brown, but those in the know will see subtle differences between them.

BREEDING COLOR

CREATING PARTICULAR COLORS

It is often difficult to predict what color a foal will be by looking at its parents. The appearance of the dam (mom) and sire (dad) will determine some of its characteristics, but others are down to chance. Purebred horses have fewer color variations. This is because some colors are more desirable than others and have been concentrated on by breeders for generations.

Contrasting colors

Palomino horses have a distinctive color combination of a golden coat with a white mane and tail. A white mane and tail on a chestnut horse is known as a "*flaxen*" mane. Contrasting colors such as these are highly sought after by breeders, and striking palomino horses regularly appear at shows, in movies, and on TV.

Growing up

Foals are usually born pale with light eyes and pinkish skin—it is only later that the adult coat color develops. Gray horses change color the most as they age. They are born a different color, such as bay or chestnut, and become gradually paler over time. Most young horses shed their baby coats at around one year old.

SOLID COLORS

ONE COLOR ALL OVER

If a horse's coat appears to be all one color, this is called a solid color, and there are many of them. A dun coat can vary from sandy yellow to reddish brown. A brown coat will have mixed black and brown hairs. Black occurs with a brown or "blue" shine. Chestnut describes shades of gold, from pale to red. Bay coats vary from red to brown with a black mane and tail.

Pure colors
True black horses are rare, but there are breeds, such as the Friesian (left), that always appear in this striking color. Other breeds may be a wide variety of colors. There are more than 100 different names in Icelandic for the colors and patterns that the Icelandic horse can have.

Chestnut Icelandic horses

MIXED COLORS

WHEN TWO COLORS MEET

Mixed coat colors appear in various different patterns. The term "pinto" describes a horse of any color with large patches of white. A roan horse has a mix of dark and light hair. Horses appear "gray" when they have a mix of black and white hair. "Snowflakes" start small and grow with age. And a "flea bitten" coat is gray with brown flecks.

Spotted horse
A horse with a spotted or "appaloosa" coat usually also has spotted skin and stripy hooves. The pattern develops as the horse matures, and may appear all over the horse's body or just around certain parts such as the hip area.

MARKINGS

WHITE PATCHES

It can be hard to tell horses apart, but white markings on their faces or legs provide useful clues. The patterns are given different names, which help when identifying individual horses. Many breed standards specify the markings that are and are not allowed, so they are also useful in identifying a horse's breed.

Face
White markings on the face are common. These include: "bald" or "white face," in which the face is white (above left); "blaze," where there is a thick line of white from forehead to nose (above middle); "star," where there is is a single point of white on the forehead (above right); and "snip"—a slither of white on the end of the nose.

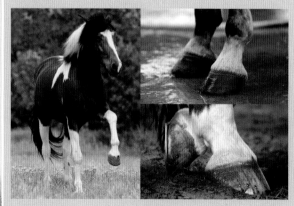

Legs
Leg markings include: "pastern," where there is white from hoof to pastern (above top right); "fetlock," which is white from hoof to fetlock (above bottom right); and "sock," which is white up to the knee. White all the way up the leg (above left) is a pattern described as "stockings."

Taming the wild

Cowboys in the US still practice skills that were developed when the
West was truly "wild." During the early 1800s, it was essential for a
cowboy to be able to rope wild Mustangs and herd cattle. Capturing
Mustang horses to sell became a way of life for some cowboys who
would spend days, or even weeks, away from home in pursuit of the
feral horses. Using the Western riding style, the cowboy controlled
his horse with the left hand, while using the lasso with the right.

WESTERN RIDING

Cowboys working long hours on ranches in North America developed the Western riding style. The style was inspired by the ranching and warfare traditions that were brought to North America by the Spanish conquistadors. Western skills and riding techniques have been adapted for competitive sports in thrilling rodeo events, such as calf-roping, steer-wrestling, barrel racing, and gymkhana.

Rounding a turn at a barrel race

Neck reining

In the Western riding style, both reins are held in the left hand (if the rider is right-handed). Aids (commands) are given to the horse by applying light pressure to the reins. Moving the hand to the left puts pressure on the right of the horse's neck, and the horse turns to the left, away from the direction of the pressure.

Chaps worn by Western rider

Leg protectors

Cowboys often wear tough leather leggings called chaps, which are buckled on over the pants. The name comes from the Spanish word *chaparreras*, after the chaparral—thick, low, thorny bushes. The chaps protect the rider's legs when passing through the bushes.

Protective, full-length chaps

Barrel racing

Barrel racing is a rodeo event for female riders. Horse and rider enter the arena at high speed and negotiate a "cloverleaf" pattern around three barrels as quickly as possible. Barrel-racing horses need to be fast, agile, and intelligent as they take tight corners around each barrel.

Lasso tied to the side

Reins kept loose

Bucking bronco

Many rodeo events are very risky for the rider. One of the most dangerous is bronc riding, in which competitors hang on to an untrained horse as it "bucks" to unseat the rider. This tests the skills that cowboys once needed to break, or train, their horses. Competitors must stay on the horse for eight seconds without touching it with their free hand. Points are awarded for more spectacular performances.

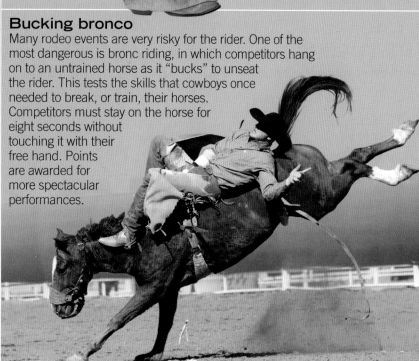

Western jog

English trot

Western or English?

In the English riding style, the rider holds one rein in each hand, and instructs the horse through the reins by pulling on the horse's mouth. The rider must learn to "post"—rising from the saddle in rhythm with the bouncy trotting gait. Western riders tend to use a slower gait called a jog, and remain in the saddle the whole time. The Western style is normally easier to learn for a novice rider.

CRIOLLO

TOUGH ARGENTINIAN PACKHORSE

The Criollo is known for its hardy nature and incredible stamina. It is tough, muscular, and able to travel long distances with very little food or water. These features make it an ideal horse for pony trekking. The Criollo's history can be traced back to the Spanish horses that were shipped to South America by early explorers in the 16th century. Their ancestors are thought to include Andalusian horses owned by Don Pedro de Mendoza, the founder of the city of Buenos Aires, Argentina.

Star marked
A white star or stripe is a common Criollo marking.

Breed name: Criollo

Other name: Argentine Criollo, Crioulo

Breed purpose: cattle farming, pleasure riding, endurance riding

Size: 14–15 hands

Coat color: variety of colors, but predominantly dun

Place of origin: Argentina

Ancestors: Andalusian, Barb, Arabian

Wild roots

The adaptable nature of the Criollo breed is a result of decades spent living wild across the lowlands of the Pampas in South America. This grassy region, stretching from the Atlantic coast to the foothills of the Andes, is where the breed thrived. Despite their wild past, Criollos are mainly used in cattle farming, pleasure riding, and long-distance trail riding.

Sturdy body
The body of a Criollo is compact and muscular, with a broad chest.

Steady gait
Typically sturdy, the Criollo has strong legs and hard-wearing hooves.

Legendary gauchos

The Criollo, with its grit and powerful build, was the mount of choice for some of the world's bravest horsemen. The cowboys of South America, the gauchos, tamed wild Criollo and used them to round up cattle. The breed became part of the folklore of South America, and many of the traditional songs, clothing, and customs were inspired by the horse.

Epic adventurer

You can't beat the Criollo for a sturdy trekking companion, and the breed is a popular choice for adventure tours. In the past, Criollos have demonstrated great feats of endurance. In 1925–28, Swiss adventurer Aimé Tschiffely led two Criollos named Mancha and Gato 13,350 miles (21,484 km) from Buenos Aires to New York. At one point, the hardy trio reached an altitude of nearly 20,000 ft (6,100 m).

Every year, **Criollos** take part in a **466-mile (750-km)** ride in Argentina, carrying **242 lbs (110 kg)** on their backs.

On a rocky high mountain pass

Built for survival

This horse survives in even the toughest climates and circumstances. It can travel vast distances and carry heavy loads, even when there is little food and water. Because of its ability to keep going in even the worst conditions, the Criollo is commonly used as a packhorse by the Argentinian army.

Trekking along a narrow trail

Coat colors

Line-backed dun (with a dark line down the back) is preferred, but the Criollo exists in various colors, including strawberry roan, black, chestnut, bay, brown, and gray.

Roan

Chestnut

Grulla (mouse-dun)

Dun

IRISH DRAFT
IRELAND'S NATIONAL BREED

The Irish Draft is an intelligent and energetic horse that is descended from the extinct Irish Hobby. Today it is recognized as the national horse of Ireland. The breed's ancestry is unclear, but it developed when warhorses from overseas, including the Spanish Andalusian, bred with native Irish stock. It is even thought by some that their ancestors swam to shore from shipwrecked Spanish galleons, which could explain the Irish Draft's resilient nature and powerful build.

Breed name: Irish Draft

Other name: Irish Draught

Breed purpose: draft work, farmwork, riding

Breed size: 15.2–17 hands

Coat color: bay, brown, gray, chestnut, black, dun

Place of origin: Ireland

Ancestors: Irish Hobby, Andalusian, Anglo-Norman breeds

As **police horses**, Irish Drafts are known for **keeping their cool** when faced with **noisy traffic** or crowds at **soccer matches**.

Irish sport horses
The Irish Draft is commonly crossed with warmbloods and Thoroughbred breeds to create a smaller, faster horse with the same gentle temperament. This cross is called the Irish Draft Sport Horse and is popularly used in racing, driving, dressage, and eventing. The Irish Hunter (Irish Draft crossed with English Thoroughbred), has a remarkable ability to jump over difficult obstacles, and excels at show jumping.

Talented farmhand
The traditional Irish Draft was bred by farmers who needed a strong, dependable horse that could do a range of jobs around the farm. The result was a gentle, powerful breed that was able to plow the land, go hunting, and pull the family trap. The Irish Draft became a familiar part of Irish rural life and was an easy addition to the family, eating mainly grass and leftover cattle feed, such as turnips and oats.

Protect and serve
Irish Draft horses are known for their docile and willing nature, as well as their robust build. For that reason, they are a popular mount for policemen in Ireland and Britain today. In the early 20th century, large numbers of Irish Drafts were also sent to the battlefields of World War I, where they were used to pull ambulances, wagons, and artillery. Many thousands lost their lives in the war.

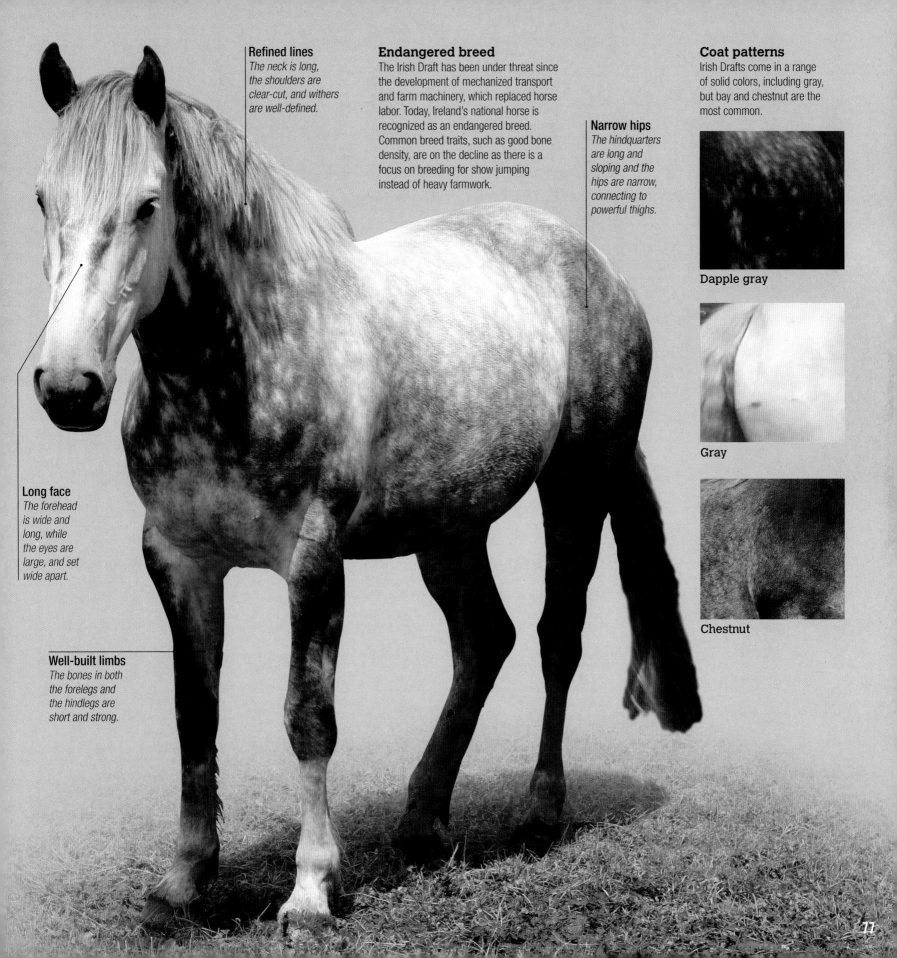

Refined lines
The neck is long, the shoulders are clear-cut, and withers are well-defined.

Endangered breed
The Irish Draft has been under threat since the development of mechanized transport and farm machinery, which replaced horse labor. Today, Ireland's national horse is recognized as an endangered breed. Common breed traits, such as good bone density, are on the decline as there is a focus on breeding for show jumping instead of heavy farmwork.

Narrow hips
The hindquarters are long and sloping and the hips are narrow, connecting to powerful thighs.

Coat patterns
Irish Drafts come in a range of solid colors, including gray, but bay and chestnut are the most common.

Dapple gray

Gray

Chestnut

Long face
The forehead is wide and long, while the eyes are large, and set wide apart.

Well-built limbs
The bones in both the forelegs and the hindlegs are short and strong.

COB

UNITED KINGDOM AND IRELAND

Before the invention of the motor car, many of the English gentry kept a Cob—a big-bodied, good-natured horse with short, powerful legs. The Cob was known to be strong and dependable, capable of pulling large loads, or carrying heavier members of a family at a hunt or on the farm. Today, Cobs are used for driving, showing, and pleasure riding.

Breed name: Cob

Other name: Gypsy Cob, Vanner, Tinker Cob, Irish Tinker

Breed purpose: riding, transportation, workhorse

Size: 15.2 hands

Coat color: any solid color, often gray, pinto

Place of origin: UK and Ireland

Ancestors: possibly Shire, Clydesdale, Dales Pony, Fell Pony, Galloway

On the road
The Gypsy Cob was first bred in the UK and Ireland by traveling people. Hard-working and reliable, it was used to pull Romani caravans. Gypsy Cobs often have feathered legs and bushy manes and tails. Black and white is a popular coloring.

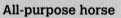

Pony-faced
The attractive head of the Cob is petite and ponylike.

All-purpose horse
This sturdily built horse is very steady, and strong enough to work as a draft horse. However, it is small, sturdy and compact, with short legs, and looks more like a large pony. Cobs come in every color and can have all kinds of marking.

River of hair
Many Cobs have a long, flowing mane.

Deep chest
A Cob has a stout, well-muscled chest.

Haunches
The haunches provide the driving strength for a steady gait.

Feathering
The long feathering on the short legs is typical of the Gypsy Cob.

Hard workers
Cobs are great working horses and are used on the farm and for forestry work. They are placid, and their calm temperament is perfect when they are called upon to do work that sometimes requires them to wait patiently for their owners.

Breed name: Welsh Cob	
Other name: Welsh pony	
Breed purpose: farmwork	
Size: 14–15 hands	
Coat color: all colors except pinto	
Place of origin: Wales	
Ancestors: Celtic ponies, Thoroughbred, Hackney, Arabian, Norfolk Roadster	

Battle horse

Ancestors of the Welsh Cob were used as warhorses as far back as the Middle Ages. The Tudor king Henry VII (1457–1509) is thought to have used Welsh Cob-like horses when he fought to regain the English throne in 1485.

WELSH COB

WALES

Today, Welsh Cobs are often used as show horses. They are particularly noted for their skills in carriage competitions. First bred in Wales, this breed was known to be an efficient farmworker and was also one of the fastest ways to get around before the advent of the motor car.

CLEVELAND BAY

UNITED KINGDOM

The Cleveland Bay is the oldest horse breed in England. These horses were once also known as "Chapman Horses," because they carried the goods of a chapman (traveling salesman) as he moved from town to town. Selective breeding later produced lighter horses, and the horse was used to pull carriages and for riding.

Breed name: Cleveland Bay	**Coat color:** bay
Other name: n/a	**Place of origin:** Yorkshire, England
Breed purpose: pack horse, carriage horse	**Ancestors:** Barb, Chapman, Andalusian
Size: 16–16.2 hands	

Coach horse

Cleveland Bays have had a long association with the British royal family. They were used as coaching horses by Queen Elizabeth I (1533–1603), and they are still used to pull carriages in royal processions today. In 1962, the current queen, Elizabeth II, bought one of the four remaining stallions, Mulgrave Supreme, and he has sired many purebred stallions.

HACKNEY

UNITED KINGDOM AND IRELAND

The Hackney was first developed in 1760 by crossing a Thoroughbred stallion, Blaze, with a Norfolk Trotter mare. Blaze, sired by the Darley Arabian racehorse, Original Shales, gave the breed speed, and this made them ideal for carriage driving on rough roads in the 1800s. Since 1878, the Hackney has become especially popular in the United States, where it is often used for competition.

Breed name: Hackney	
Other name: n/a	
Breed purpose: carriage horse, driving, competition	
Size: 14.2–16.2 hands	
Coat color: bay, brown, chestnut, black	
Place of origin: UK and Ireland	
Ancestors: Norfolk Trotter, Darley Arabian, Thoroughbred	

Riding style

The Hackney is high-stepping, a trait inherited from its trotting horse ancestors. It makes a great carriage horse. It can be driven as a single horse or in teams of two, three, or four.

KNABSTRUPPER

STRIKING DANISH WARMBLOOD

The colorful coat and unusual spotted markings makes this eye-catching breed stand out. Thought to be of Spanish ancestry, the Knabstrupper can be traced back to a chestnut mare called Fläbehoppen that was crossed with a Frederiksborg stallion. Fläbehoppen was known for her speed and endurance, as well as her beautiful appearance—a dark red coat with white "snowflakes" on the body, and flowing white mane and tail.

Breed name: Knabstrupper

Other name: Knabstrup

Breed purpose: harness work, dressage, eventing, show jumping

Breed size: 15.2–16 hands

Coat color: spotted, in a variety of colors

Place of origin: Zealand, Denmark

Ancestors: Frederiksborg, Spanish horses

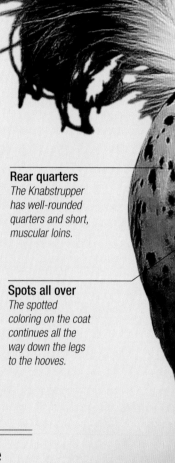

Tail carriage
The bloodline is reflected in the flowing tail.

Rear quarters
The Knabstrupper has well-rounded quarters and short, muscular loins.

Spots all over
The spotted coloring on the coat continues all the way down the legs to the hooves.

Easy to spot
The Knabstrupper is easy to spot because of its colorful coat, but this hasn't always been in its favor. During the Schleswig War in Denmark (1848–50), Knabstruppers were used as cavalry mounts for Danish officers. Unfortunately, their unusual markings made them easy targets for enemy snipers.

Tip-top talent
Today, these versatile riding horses are valued for their ability across dressage, eventing, and show jumping. As they are naturally small horses, they also make good-natured riding ponies for children. This rare and talented breed needs to be protected because only 600 are known to exist worldwide.

Knabstruppers have been **crossed** with **Trakehners** and **Danish Warmbloods** to produce **taller**, more **athletic** horses that excel at **sports**.

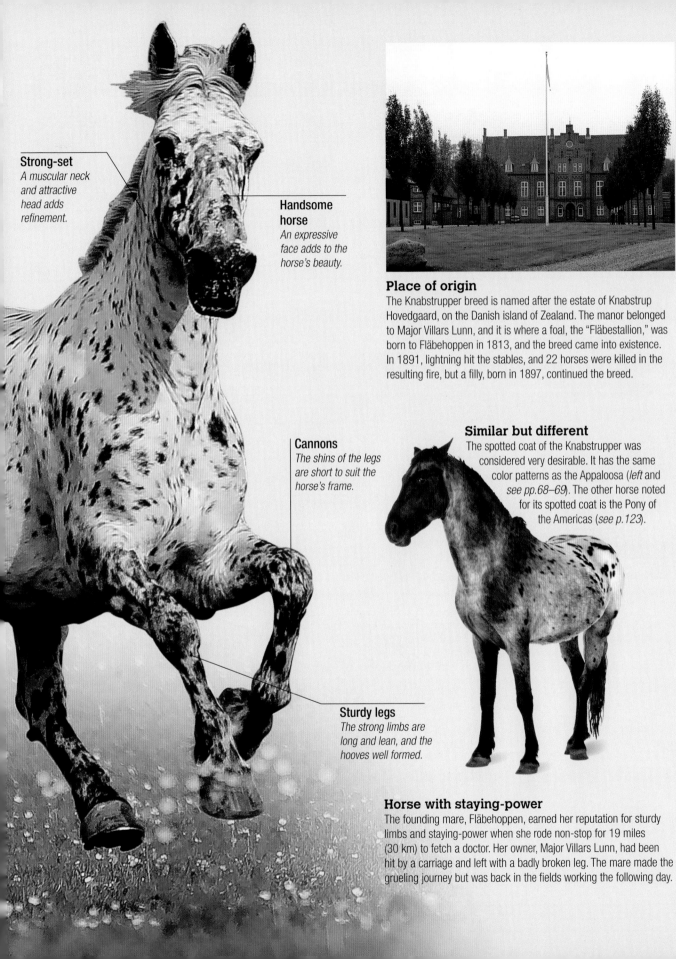

Strong-set
A muscular neck and attractive head adds refinement.

Handsome horse
An expressive face adds to the horse's beauty.

Cannons
The shins of the legs are short to suit the horse's frame.

Sturdy legs
The strong limbs are long and lean, and the hooves well formed.

Place of origin

The Knabstrupper breed is named after the estate of Knabstrup Hovedgaard, on the Danish island of Zealand. The manor belonged to Major Villars Lunn, and it is where a foal, the "Fläbestallion," was born to Fläbehoppen in 1813, and the breed came into existence. In 1891, lightning hit the stables, and 22 horses were killed in the resulting fire, but a filly, born in 1897, continued the breed.

Similar but different

The spotted coat of the Knabstrupper was considered very desirable. It has the same color patterns as the Appaloosa (*left* and *see pp.68–69*). The other horse noted for its spotted coat is the Pony of the Americas (*see p.123*).

Horse with staying-power

The founding mare, Fläbehoppen, earned her reputation for sturdy limbs and staying-power when she rode non-stop for 19 miles (30 km) to fetch a doctor. Her owner, Major Villars Lunn, had been hit by a carriage and left with a badly broken leg. The mare made the grueling journey but was back in the fields working the following day.

Coat colors

Knabstruppers come in a huge variety of colors to accompany their iconic spots. The most common color pattern is the leopard and other patterns include the blanket, the snowflake, and the snowcap.

Bay leopard

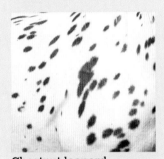

Chestnut leopard

Snowflake

Few spot leopard

Winter wonderland

Although it is usually a small light-colored horse, the Knabstrupper from Denmark (*see pp. 80–81*) is tough, with powerful shoulders, a strong neck, muscular body, and stout limbs. With these characteristics, it makes an excellent carriage horse that is still used to pull traditional carts during winter months in Wildbad Kreuth in Germany. The breed's stamina is legendary. One Knabstrupper colt called Mikkel, born in 1818, would pull a carriage 25 miles (40 km) to a racetrack before winning races. He was defeated only once, when he was 16 years old!

FRIESIAN

THE NETHERLANDS

The ancestors of this horse lived in the northern Friesland area of the Netherlands for centuries. Their large size enabled them to carry knights in heavy armor, so they were in great demand as warhorses. Competition from heavier horses led their numbers to drop almost to extinction by the mid-20th century. Fortunately, a few horses survived and their numbers have since increased considerably.

High steps
With its brisk, high-stepping trot, a Friesian horse pulling a carriage makes an impressive sight. In recent years, as its numbers have recovered, the breed has become increasingly popular in driving competitions and dressage.

Camera-ready
The striking appearance of the Friesian has led to the breed making regular appearances on the big and small screen. The horse's glossy black color, powerful neck, and impressive looks work exceptionally well on camera, and Friesians are a top choice among film makers. Movies and TV shows that feature Friesians include *The Chronicles of Narnia*, *The Mask of Zorro*, and *Game of Thrones*.

Breed name: Friesian

Other name: Belgian Black

Breed purpose: farmwork, riding, racing

Size: 15.3 hands

Coat color: black

Place of origin: Friesland, Netherlands

Ancestors: local forest horse, Arabian, Andalusian

Movie star looks
The horse has a well-muscled, shimmering black body.

Strong base
The legs are short and strong, with light feathering on the withers.

DANISH WARMBLOOD

DENMARK

Created in 1962, the Danish Warmblood was Denmark's first riding horse. Danish horses were crossed with Thoroughbreds, Frederiksborgs, and Anglo-Norman breeds to produce a horse with strength, elegance, and stamina. The new breed quickly won many fans around the world.

Breed name: Danish Warmblood

Other name: n/a

Breed purpose: riding, farm work, competition

Size: 16.2 hands

Coat color: any solid color, white markings common

Place of origin: Denmark

Ancestors: Groningen, Gelderlander, Frederiksborg, Thoroughbred, Anglo-Norman horse, Trakehner

Thoroughbred lines
The breed has the elegant shape of its Thoroughbred ancestors, which is combined with a solid build and strong legs.

Young breed
The well-balanced structure of the Danish Warmblood make it an exceptional competition horse. It is still a relatively young breed and Danish breeders have worked hard to promote the horse and showcase some of the best stallions at various competitions in Denmark. Every year, the Stallion of the Year award is presented to the stallion that has sired the finest offspring.

Show head
The well-proportioned head is typical of horses that are successful in dressage competitions.

Champion horses
The Danish Warmblood breed is suited to dressage, cross-country, and show jumping (left). The breed was developed specifically for sports, and is seen at competitive events worldwide. Dutch rider Albert Voorn won a silver medal for show jumping at the Sydney Olympics in 2000 on a Danish Warmblood stallion named Lando. A year earlier, the Danish Warmblood gelding Marzog had been named Dressage Horse of the Century.

HAFLINGER

TYROLEAN MOUNTAIN BREED

Highly sought after for its dependable nature, the Haflinger's ancestors are thought to date back to medieval times. The modern breed takes its name from the mountain district of Hafling, Italy, and is descended from the Arabian stallion El Bedavi. Brought to the region in the 19th century, the stallion was crossed with a beautiful alpine mare, leading to the birth of the foundation stallion "249 Folie."

Family horse
The Haflinger is known for its willing and friendly nature. Living and working in remote alpine regions, the horse would become an integral part of the family it lived with. It carried out a variety of jobs, including draft, pack, and agricultural tasks. To this day, it is considered a versatile and gentle breed that gets along well with people.

Breed name: Haflinger

Other names: Avelignese

Breed purpose: draft, pack, and agricultural work, pleasure riding, driving

Size: 13–15 hands

Coat color: chestnut, palomino

Place of origin: Austria

Ancestors: Arabian, European, native Tyrolean

Marked by a star
From the 1970s onward, strict breeding standards were introduced with the aim of developing a lighter-framed horse that could be used for driving and riding. After a rigorous inspection process, successful horses are branded with the traditional edelweiss mark. The edelweiss flower is commonly associated with the Alps, and this branding is a unique symbol of the breed's alpine heritage.

The star-shaped edelweiss flower

Flaxen mane
One of the Haflinger's stand-out features is its beautiful, pale mane and tail.

Hardy history
Traditionally reared on high mountain pastures where the air is thin, such as this one in the Tyrol, Italy, the Haflinger has developed a strong heart and large lungs. It is also a sure-footed breed, and very capable in steep and dangerous mountain landscapes. These traits make the Haflinger an ideal trekking horse that has endurance, stability, and control.

Refined build
Strength and elegance combine to make the Haflinger a great riding horse.

Haflinger feeding on summer grass

In **2008**, Italian scientists produced the world's first **cloned horse**— a Haflinger named **Prometea**.

Made for the mountains

With its roots in the Alps of Austria and Italy, the Haflinger is perfectly at home in the harsh winters of mountainous regions. Its strong build and hardy nature make it ideal to carry out work on alpine farms. Since the end of World War II, many breeders have also developed the qualities needed for an easy-going riding horse, creating a taller, leaner version of the breed.

End of a line

Outside Churchill Downs racecourse in Kentucky, US, stands a statue of the 2006 Kentucky Derby winner Barbaro. This popular stallion had an impressive pedigree that included the champion horses Raise a Native, and Mr. Prospector. Barbaro died following an accident shortly after winning the Derby, aged just 3, which meant that he was not able to sire his own line of champions.

BREEDS AND STUD BOOKS

Stud books, or breed registries, are official records in which the parents of each new foal are recorded. Breeders register their foals with the stud book and are given a certificate that confirms the horse's ancestry and breed. Some stud books are "closed," and only foals with two parents of the right breed can be registered. Others are "open," and any horse with the right set of characteristics can be registered.

Out to stud
A mare can only breed for a few weeks each year, in a period known as the *estrous cycle*. Successful racehorses are in high demand for breeding, and the owners of mares may pay fees of up to $1 million to have their foals sired by a top Thoroughbred stallion. The foal is born after about 11 months.

American Stud Book
The *American Stud Book* was first compiled in 1868 by noted horse breeder Sanders D. Bruce. Now published by the Jockey Club, it documents all Thoroughbred horses born in the United States, Canada, and Puerto Rico. It's a serious business, with genetic testing carried out to confirm parentage and resolve disputes between owners. Only horses on the register are permitted to race.

AMERICAN JOCKEY CLUB RACES, JEROME PARK.

Thoroughbred race in New York (1873) just after first US stud book was published

A mare and stallion meet

Thoroughbred foal with a distinctive white patch that will be recorded in the registry

Registering a foal
Each stud book registration is different and will have various requirements in place to help maintain breed standards. This often includes: a certificate confirming registration to a breed society that is also part of the World Breeding Federation; a diagram of the horse's distinguishable features, completed by a vet; printed copies of the sire and dam's pedigree status. Occasionally, DNA samples are needed, using a hair taken from the mane or tail of the horse.

Registering cross-breeds
Some stud books are "semi-open" and allow cross-breeds with desirable traits to be registered. These horses are recorded in a separate book, and their offspring can be transferred to the main book after passing performance tests. In this way, the standard of the breed is maintained but new blood lines are allowed, sometimes enhancing the breed. The American Quarter Horse Association is the largest registry in the world and admits Quarter Horse and Thoroughbred crosses.

Champion sire
Affectionately known as "Big Red," Man o' War was one of the most successful racehorses ever. In his two-year racing career, he won 20 out of the 21 races he started. Big Red sired many champion horses, including winners of the Kentucky Derby and the Grand National. Breeders often arrange matings with descendants of Man o' War because of his celebrated reputation.

Statue of Man o' War at the Kentucky Horse Park

Man o' War in 1920

Paint Horse, a Quarter Horse and Thoroughbred cross

WÜRTTEMBERGER
GERMANY

The Württemberger is one of the oldest German warmbloods, developed at the Marbach stud in southwestern Germany. Since the 17th century, Württembergers have only been bred at the Marbach stud. This reliable breed has an excellent temperament and performs well in show jumping and dressage competitions.

Breed name: Württemberger	Coat color: bay, brown, black or chestnut
Other name: Baden-Württemberger	Place of origin: Germany
Breed purpose: competitions such as show jumping and dressage	Ancestors: Arabian, Anglo-Norman, Barb, Suffolk Punch, Spanish, Friesian, Trakehner
Breed size: 16 hands	

Versatile breed
The early Württemberger established a reputation as a good utility horse, suitable for riding and harness work. The breed made useful farm horses in Germany, capable of doing a variety of jobs. The horses are still used for light draft work and can be seen pulling carriages at local German festivals.

Sportier version
In the 1950s, breeders wanted a lighter, athletic build—one that was more suited to competitions. As a result, a notable Trakehner stallion called Julmond was introduced. Other breeds were also used to help further refine the Württemberger and create stronger, faster horses.

EINSIEDLER
SWITZERLAND

This horse has its origins at the Benedictine Monastery of Einsiedeln, a place noted for breeding riding horses ever since the 11th century. Einsiedlers have expressive faces and strong builds, which reflect their Anglo-Norman bloodlines.

Strong and solid
Large and powerfully built, the Einsiedler is a good all-round performer.

Breed name: Einsiedler	Coat color: all solid colors
Other names: Swiss Warmblood, Swiss Half-Bred	Place of origin: Switzerland
Breed purpose: general riding, sports, cavalry, driving	Ancestors: Anglo-Norman, Holsteiner, Swedish horses, Yorkshire Coach
Breed size: 16.2 hands	

Cavalry to competition
The Einsiedler breed was developed in the 19th century in response to a growing demand for strong cavalry horses. Today, its athletic qualities are put to use in competition, and it is successful in dressage, show jumping, cross country, and driving.

TRAKEHNER

LITHUANIA

With an intelligent, willing temperament and athletic build, the Trakehner is a popular sports horse with an impressive international record. Originally from East Prussia (modern-day Lithuania), the Trakehner shares bloodlines with Arabian, Thoroughbred, and Turk breeds. These ancestors strengthened the Trakehner line, developing a horse with a robust constitution and hardy nature, which lent itself well to cavalry work.

Breed name: Trakehner

Other name: The East Prussian Warmblood Horse of Trakehner Descent

Breed purpose: riding, sports, dressage, shows

Size: 16–17 hands

Coat color: any solid color

Place of origin: Lithuania

Ancestors: Arab, Thoroughbred, Schweiken, Turkomen

Strong joints
The well-formed legs have very strong joints, which add to the robust nature of the breed.

Handsome head
The finely shaped head has well-spaced eyes and narrows at the muzzle.

Show business
The Trakehner's slim build, muscular structure, and graceful posture make it one of the most common show horses in Germany. The breed's intelligence, alert nature, and stable gait make it a popular riding horse.

Stallion galloping in the paddock

Strong shoulders
The well-shaped, sloping shoulders give this horse an easy movement.

Trakehner in spring pasture

Hardy sports horse
The Trakehners of today can all be traced back to a few hundred horses that remained after World War II. The animals were pushed to the limits of endurance by the German army, and only the strongest and fittest survived. Their offspring have since become renowned as hardy, brave horses with excellent movement that are well suited to a variety of equine sports.

LIPIZZANER
ELEGANT RIDING HORSE

The Lipizzaner is famous for its controlled and stuntlike jumps and movements, known as "airs above the ground." These spectacular moves are honed at the Spanish Riding School in Vienna, Austria, where the horses train and give public performances. The breed dates back to the 16th century, when the Hapsburg monarchy, rulers of both Spain and Austria, wanted a new and elegant horse. The name Lipizzaner comes from Lipica (Lipizza) in Slovenia, where the horse was first bred.

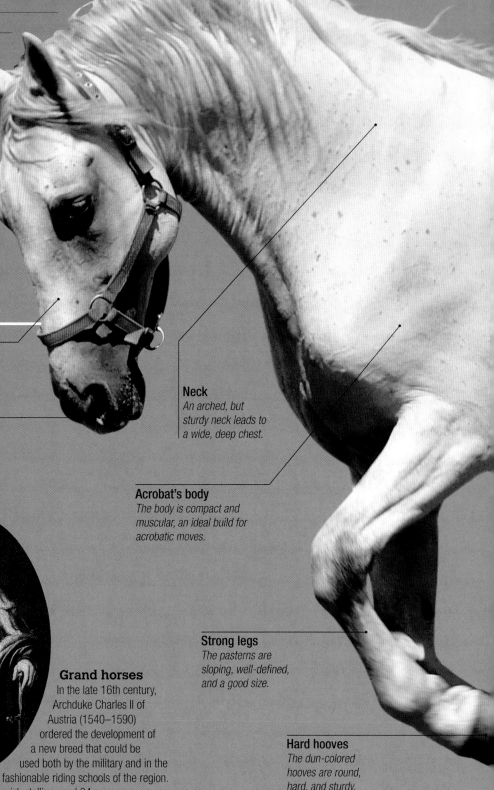

Breed name: Lipizzaner

Other names: Lipizzan

Breed purpose: military use, ceremonial occasions, dressage

Breed size: 14–16 hands

Coat color: any solid color, mostly gray

Place of origin: Slovenia

Ancestors: Spanish, Neapolitan, Arabian, Barb

Face
The well-shaped head of the Lipizzaner is long and it has expressive eyes.

Flaring nostrils
The large nostrils are flared regularly.

Neck
An arched, but sturdy neck leads to a wide, deep chest.

Acrobat's body
The body is compact and muscular, an ideal build for acrobatic moves.

Strong legs
The pasterns are sloping, well-defined, and a good size.

Hard hooves
The dun-colored hooves are round, hard, and sturdy.

Taking off
The famous "airs above the ground" performed by the Lipizzaner require incredible muscle strength and control. There are seven types of airs. These include the *levade* (above), in which a horse raises up both front legs so that it is standing entirely on its hind legs.

Grand horses
In the late 16th century, Archduke Charles II of Austria (1540–1590) ordered the development of a new breed that could be used both by the military and in the fashionable riding schools of the region. Nine Spanish stallions and 24 mares were imported from Spain and Portugal.

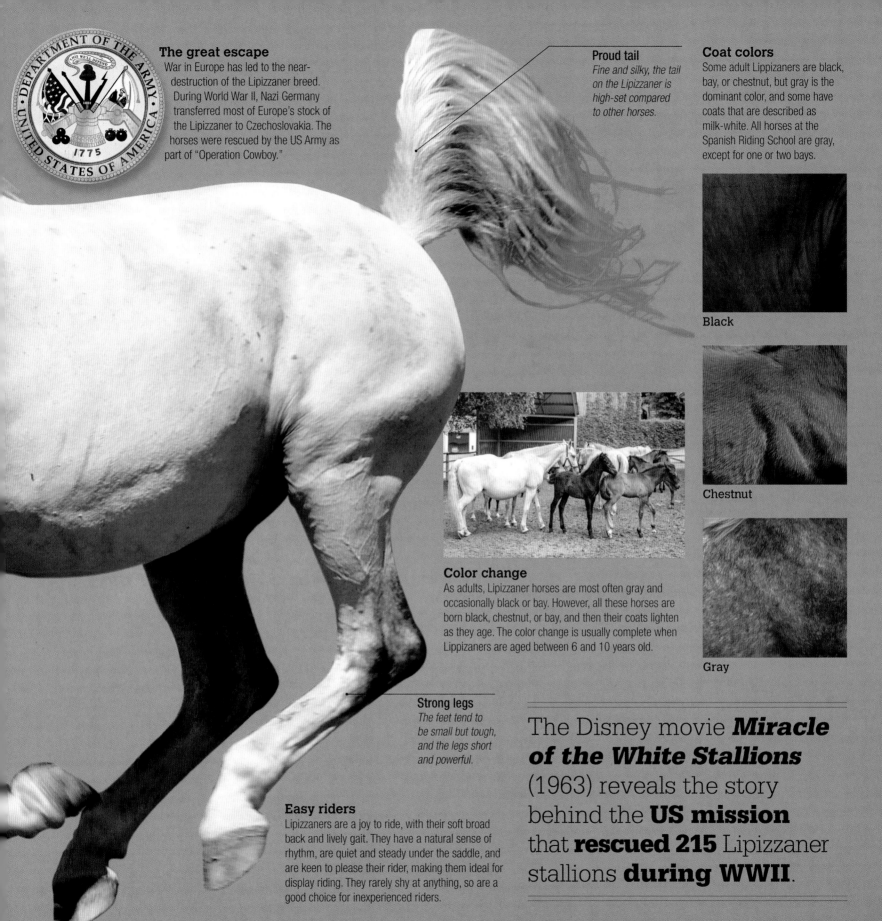

The great escape
War in Europe has led to the near-destruction of the Lipizzaner breed. During World War II, Nazi Germany transferred most of Europe's stock of the Lipizzaner to Czechoslovakia. The horses were rescued by the US Army as part of "Operation Cowboy."

Proud tail
Fine and silky, the tail on the Lipizzaner is high-set compared to other horses.

Coat colors
Some adult Lipizzaners are black, bay, or chestnut, but gray is the dominant color, and some have coats that are described as milk-white. All horses at the Spanish Riding School are gray, except for one or two bays.

Black

Chestnut

Gray

Color change
As adults, Lipizzaner horses are most often gray and occasionally black or bay. However, all these horses are born black, chestnut, or bay, and then their coats lighten as they age. The color change is usually complete when Lipizzaners are aged between 6 and 10 years old.

Strong legs
The feet tend to be small but tough, and the legs short and powerful.

Easy riders
Lipizzaners are a joy to ride, with their soft broad back and lively gait. They have a natural sense of rhythm, are quiet and steady under the saddle, and are keen to please their rider, making them ideal for display riding. They rarely shy at anything, so are a good choice for inexperienced riders.

The Disney movie **Miracle of the White Stallions** (1963) reveals the story behind the **US mission** that **rescued 215** Lipizzaner stallions **during WWII**.

Airs above the ground

The spectacular dressage "airs above the ground" movements and jumps of the amazing Lippizaners of the Spanish Riding School in Vienna were originally designed to entertain the nobles and then to improve the strength and agility of military horses. Over time, the moves have developed into what is now an extraordinary ballet set to classical music that travels all over the world to acclaim from its center in Vienna. Moves like this one take many years to perfect, and are extremely demanding of both horse and rider.

ANDALUSIAN

MAJESTIC BREED FROM SOUTHERN SPAIN

The elegant and noble Andalusian is descended from the Iberian horses of Spain and Portugal. Its name is taken from the Spanish region of Andalusia. Probably a cross between a Sorraia (*see p.138*) and a North-African Barb (*see pp.38–39*), the breed was founded after 1476 by monks at a Spanish monastery. By the 19th century, the Andalusian was Europe's premier horse, its high-stepping walk and stately appearance a sign of true quality.

Breed name: Andalusian

Other name: Pure Spanish Horse or PRE (Pura Raza Espanola)

Breed purpose: riding, driving, military use, performance

Size: 15–17 hands

Coat color: mostly bay and gray

Place of origin: Andalusia, Spain

Ancestors: Iberian horses, Sorraia, Barb

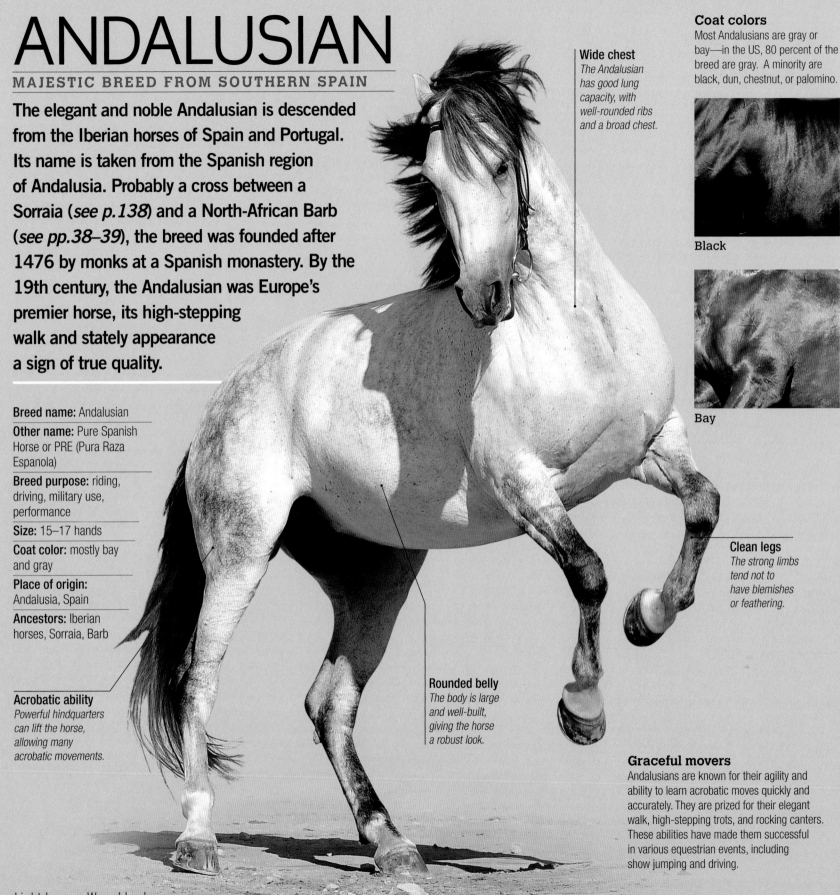

Coat colors
Most Andalusians are gray or bay—in the US, 80 percent of the breed are gray. A minority are black, dun, chestnut, or palomino.

Black

Bay

Wide chest
The Andalusian has good lung capacity, with well-rounded ribs and a broad chest.

Clean legs
The strong limbs tend not to have blemishes or feathering.

Acrobatic ability
Powerful hindquarters can lift the horse, allowing many acrobatic movements.

Rounded belly
The body is large and well-built, giving the horse a robust look.

Graceful movers
Andalusians are known for their agility and ability to learn acrobatic moves quickly and accurately. They are prized for their elegant walk, high-stepping trots, and rocking canters. These abilities have made them successful in various equestrian events, including show jumping and driving.

Two **Andalusians**, Blanco and Domero, played **Gandalf's** stallion, **Shadowfax**, in two of the **Lord of the Rings** films.

Carthusian cousin
The purest strain of an Andalusian horse is believed to be the Carthusian. They are fairly rare and are thought to be descended from a magnificent gray stallion named Esclavo that lived in the 18th century. Esclavo is said to have had warts under his tail, a trait that he passed on to his offspring.

Fine features
The head is light and elegant, with expressive, alert eyes.

Tail carriage
A low-set and luxuriant tail flows behind the horse as it moves.

Fit for kings
As early as the 15th century, Spanish horses were given as gifts to royal monarchs across Europe. King Henry VIII of England received Spanish horses from the Spanish monarchy when he married Catherine of Aragon in 1509. Statues and portraits of the kings of France, such as King Louis XIV (1638–1715, above), often showed royalty riding Spanish-style horses.

Dressage performance

Bullring in Spain

Show horse
In Spain, the Andalusian has historically been used as bullfighter's steed. With its high-kicking pace, the breed excels in sports, and was one of the first used in dressage. It is now a medal-winning competition horse worldwide.

ELITE DRESSAGE

ELEGANT AND AGILE SPORTS BREEDS

Some horse breeds perform particularly well at dressage, alongside other sporting disciplines, such as show jumping. To excel at dressage, a horse and its rider must display exceptional control and balance, mastering complex maneuvers, from diagonal or lateral (sideways) movements to long strides when cantering. These give the appearance of a spectacular gymnastic display or an elegant dance.

Perfect poise
One of the display moves of these elite horses in dressage is the high-stepping trot. In this, diagonal pairs of legs move forward together.

DUTCH WARMBLOOD

THE NETHERLANDS

Dutch Warmbloods are the product of a strict breeding program. In the 1960s, two Dutch breeds, Gelderlander and Groningen, were crossed with Thoroughbreds and other breeds to create one of the most successful competition horses in Europe. It is known as an athletic breed with good stamina and a reputation for working in harmony with a rider.

Breed name: Dutch Warmblood

Other name: n/a

Breed purpose: competition, sport

Size: 16 hands

Coat color: bay, brown, black, gray

Place of origin: Holland

Ancestors: Gelderlander, Groningen, Thoroughbred, French and German warmbloods

Rearing lion
The hindquarters of Dutch Warmbloods were once branded with the image of a lion in a shield, a symbol found on the Netherlands' royal coat of arms (right). Branding is now illegal in the Netherlands, so today Dutch Warmbloods are microchipped.

Going for gold
The Dutch Warmblood breed is known for its talent in dressage and show jumping, winning gold medals at the Olympics and on the international stage. It is attractively proportioned, easy to train, and intelligent.

Sporting star
The most common coat color for the Selle Français is chestnut. It has a lively, spirited temperament, and a well-balanced gait.

OLDENBURG

GERMANY

The Oldenburg was established in Germany in the 17th century almost solely by one man, Count Anton Gunther von Oldenburg. It was originally bred as a powerful horse capable of pulling carriages, but with the introduction of motor cars in the 20th century, the breeding focus changed to create a modern riding horse.

Breed name: Oldenburg

Other name: Oldenburger

Breed purpose: carriage work and riding

Size: 16.2–17.2 hands

Coat color: brown, black, bay, gray

Place of origin: Oldenburg, Germany

Ancestors: various European breeds, Arabian, Barb

Competition horse
The Oldenburg excels in dressage and show jumping and has a rhythmic and expressive gait. Despite a history as a carriage horse, the modern-day Oldenburg is bred purely for riding and competitions.

SELLE FRANÇAIS

FRANCE

Development of the Selle Français began in 19th century France when native mares were crossed with heavier breeds. In 1958, these horses were grouped together under one name, Selle Français. The breed has achieved success in show jumping, dressage, and eventing.

Breed name: Selle Francais

Other name: French Saddle horse

Breed purpose: riding and competition

Size: over 16 hands

Coat color: usually chestnut, bay, brown

Place of origin: Normandy, France

Ancestors: Thoroughbred, Norfolk Roadster, French Trotter, Anglo-Norman

PASO FINO

SOUTH AMERICA

These refined and gentle horses are the descendants of horses first brought to the Americas by the Spanish conquistadors from the 16th century onward. Its ancestry also includes the Spanish Jennet, a breed brought to the Caribbean by the explorer Christopher Columbus.

Smooth ride
Paso Fino name means "fine step," and the horse is famed for its uniquely smooth and natural gait. It is an evenly-spaced four-beat lateral gait in which each foot contacts the ground separately and evenly in sequence. As a result, the rider appears almost motionless.

Breed name: Paso Fino

Other name: Los Caballos de Los Paso Fino

Breed purpose: plantation work

Breed size: 13–15.2 hands

Coat color: all colors

Place of origin: South America

Ancestors: Peruvian Paso, Barb, Spanish Jennet, Andalusian

A proud breed

The Salerno breed was heavily influenced by Lipizzaner stock, a refined and noble gray breed that was commonly used for ceremonies and royal events (*see pp.92–93*). Three foundation sires, Pluto, Conversano, and Napoletano, were developed into a quality riding horse. Unfortunately the Salerno is a rare breed today, despite its success as a riding horse and showjumper.

SALERNO

SPORTING WARMBLOOD

Reliable, athletic, and with a talent for show jumping, the Salerno is probably the best of the Italian riding horses. The breed was developed in the late 18th century in the beautiful Campania region of southwestern Italy. The Salerno stands out as one of the most attractive Italian warmbloods, an elegant and fiery horse, influenced by Spanish and Barb breeds, that is recognized as an exceptional sports horse.

Home territory
The horse is named after the town of Salerno (above). The horse was developed for cavalry use, and it became renowned for its intelligence and strength—qualities that have led to its success in top-level sports.

Breed name: Salerno

Other names: Salernitano

Breed purpose: jumping, racing, riding, work, polo

Breed size: 16 hands

Coat color: black, bay, gray, chestnut

Place of origin: Italy

Ancestors: Neapolitan, Thoroughbred, Arabian, Andalusian, Lipizzaner

Frozen in time
The importance of horses in the province of Salerno can be traced to the 3rd century BCE. The region is home to the ancient Greek city of Paestum—an incredible historical site that contains artifacts from Greek, Lucanian, and Roman periods. This painted fresco, showing a chariot pulled by the ancestors of the Salerno, dates to around 350 BCE and was found in the tomb of Lucan in Paestum.

Arabian competing at the Arabian Horse Show

Persano horses taking part in a parade

Sporting heroes
Salernos have been hugely successful in equestrian sports and have won some top prizes. Two of the most famous are Merano and Posillipo, ridden by the Italian show jumper, Raimondo D'Inzeo. Riding Merano (right), D'Inzeo won a gold medal at the World Championship in 1956. In 1960, he won a gold medal at the Rome Olympics riding Posillipo.

Blood lines
The Salerno was first bred, alongside the Persano horse, at the Persano stud, founded in 1763 by the king of Naples, Charles III. The Salerno was based on the Neapolitan breed and has the poise of its Arab ancestors, which is why the town is home to the prestigious Arabian Horse Show. Lipizzaners (*see pp.92–93*) were crossed with local horses to create a quality riding horse and talented show horse.

Teamwork is best

A good relationship between horse and rider is vital, and never more so than when tackling the sometimes terrifying jumps in competitive shows. The match has to be an equal one—a top showjumper that works well with a professional rider will not suit the amateur or inexperienced rider. The recipe for success is the horse that has the right balance between ability and temperament, and is trainable and willing to work hard. This successful showjumping pair is taking part in a competition at a horse carnival in Selangor, Malaysia.

SHOW JUMPERS

ATHLETIC WARMBLOODS

Champion show jumping horses need to be strong, athletic, and fearless to clear fences that may be up to 5 feet (1.55 meters) in height. They also need to be able to take sharp turns and accelerate quickly around the course to avoid time penalties. The best show jumpers are normally at least 16 hands tall, but smaller horses have also found success.

SWEDISH WARMBLOOD

SWEDEN

Sweden has a long tradition of equestrian sports and a reputation for producing high-quality competition horses. Descended from a variety of breeds imported into Sweden from the 17th century, the Swedish Warmblood is a tall, powerful horse that has proved hugely successful in show jumping, dressage, and eventing.

Breed name: Swedish Warmblood
Other name: Anglo-Arabian
Breed purpose: riding
Size: 16.2 hands
Coat color: any solid color
Places of origin: Sweden
Ancestors: Thoroughbred, Hanoverian, Arab, Trakehner

Grueling tests

Swedish breeders ensure that foals graze on high-quality pasture so that they grow up strong. Mares and stallions are given athletic performance tests before they are allowed to breed. The result is a horse with an exceptional shape and strength.

Able horse

The breed varies considerably in color, size, and build, as breeders consider the horse's abilities more important than its looks. It must be willing and able to jump high and far, and also have a strong desire not to touch the bars on the way over!

BELGIAN WARMBLOOD

BELGIUM

This sport horse was developed in Belgium from the 1950s. Careful breeding has produced an athletic but calm horse that is ideally suited to the challenges of top-level show jumping. With champion jumpers such as Big Ben, the breed has enjoyed huge success in recent years, fulfilling the promise of the Belgian Warmblood Stud's motto "Bred to Perform."

Mare and foal grazing

Swedish warmblood Pimliko in competition

Breed name: Belgian Warmblood	Coat color: any solid color
	Place of origin: Belgium
Other name: Belgian Sport Horse	Ancestors: Gelderlander, Hanoverian, Holsteiner, Selle Français, Thoroughbred, Anglo-Arab
Breed purpose: show jumping	
Breed size: 16.2 hands	

WESTPHALIAN
GERMANY

Bred at the State Stud in Warendorf in the 19th century, this horse is one of the top breeds in show jumping and dressage, and is popular with both professional and amateur riders. Calm but bold, and with a long, athletic gait, the Westphalian is a strong all-round sports horse, and more recently it has found success in North American show hunting competitions.

Breed name: Westphalian
Other name: Westfalen
Breed purpose: riding, competition
Size: 15.2–17.2 hands
Coat color: all colors permitted
Place of origin: Germany
Ancestors: Thoroughbred, Rhineland coldbloods

Long jump
The Westphalian has achieved most success in dressage, but it is also an Olympic-level show jumper. It has an exceptionally long stride, which helps it to clear large obstacles, such as the water jump.

HOLSTEINER
GERMANY

Thought to be the oldest warmblood breed in Germany, the Holsteiner traces its ancestry back to the 13th century and the windswept marshes of northern Germany. In 1891, breeders in the Holstein area came together to improve the breed, introducing Thoroughbred and English coach horse lines. Today, the Holsteiner is renowned worldwide for its jumping skills.

Breed name: Holsteiner
Other name: n/a
Breed purpose: coach horse, sports horse
Size: 16–17 hands
Coat color: any solid color
Place of origin: Schleswig-Holstein, Germany
Ancestors: local horses, Thoroughbred, Yorkshire Coach

Change of mood
Holsteiners vary greatly in their temperament. Calm, cooperative horses are favored by amateurs, while professional riders prefer animals that are bold and sensitive.

HANOVERIAN
GERMANY

An all-round competitor that has won Olympic gold medals in show jumping, dressage, and three-day eventing, the Hanoverian was originally bred to pull coaches. The breed was established in 1735 at the Celle State Stud in northern Germany, which had been set up by the British King George II. Celle remains a major center for the Hanoverian, but it is also bred in North America, South America, Australia, and New Zealand.

Breed name: Hanoverian
Other name: Hannoveraner
Breed purpose: originally a coach horse, now sports
Size: 15.3–16.2 hands
Coat color: any solid color
Place of origin: Celle, northern Germany
Ancestors: Thoroughbred, Spanish, Trakehner, Neopolitan, Holsteiner

Good mover
Today's Hanoverian is a high-quality competition horse. It retains the sturdy build of its carriage-pulling days, but combines this with a light, free movement.

In training

Hanoverian at full gallop

CZECH WARMBLOOD

CZECH REPUBLIC

The original purpose of this breed was to serve as a cavalry horse, and today it is considered a solid, uncomplicated horse that is a safe mount for inexperienced riders. With mixed ancestry, there is no single type to the breed, but it typically has low, broad withers, which is a sign of its Arabian blood.

Slimline
The slim, arching neck leads to low-slung shoulders.

A palomino Czech Warmblood

Breed name: Czech Warmblood
Other name: n/a
Breed purpose: riding, sport
Size: 16–16.2 hands
Coat color: any solid color
Place of origin: Czech Republic
Ancestors: various, including Furioso, Nonius, Shagya Arab

Czech Warmblood jumping

Riding school breed
The Czech Warmblood has a calm, easy-going nature and is very popular in riding schools. It has a smart appearance and can be trained to perform show jumping and dressage, but does not have the precise steps of a top-quality dressage breed.

WIELKOPOLSKI

POLAND

Developed by crossing two now-extinct Polish breeds, the Poznan and the Masuren, the Wiekopolski is a strong, well-balanced competition horse. Lighter types are popular in show jumping and dressage, while heavier horses are used under harness.

Breed name: Wielkopolski
Other name: n/a
Breed purpose: riding and farmwork, eventing
Size: 15.2–16.2 hands
Coat color: all solid colors
Place of origin: Poland
Ancestors: Arabian, Thoroughbred, Trakehner, Hanoverian

Fearless performer
The influence of Thoroughbred blood is clearly seen in the Wielkopolski, which has the speed, stamina, and courage to compete in cross-country competitions, as well as being a very good show jumper.

HUNGARIAN WARMBLOOD

HUNGARY

Founded in 1784 by the Mezohegyes State Stud in Hungary, this well-built breed has found success in a range of sports events, most notably in show jumping. Since the end of World War II, it has also been bred in the United States, where a strict breeding standard is maintained in order to produce top-class sporting horses.

Breed name: Hungarian Warmblood

Other name: Hungarian Sport Horse, Mezőhegyes Sport Horse

Breed purpose: sports, riding

Size: 16.2–17 hands

Coat color: all solid colors

Place of origin: Hungary

Ancestors: mixed, Hungarian breeds

White face
This breed commonly has a white blaze on its face.

Specialized breeding
Several types of Hungarian Warmblood are selectively bred, each one specializing in a different sports event. In the past, the breed has won top-class show jumping competitions.

FURIOSO

HUNGARY

This breed is named after the foundation stallion, Furioso (born 1836), and a second influential Thoroughbred stallion, North Star (born 1844). In 1885, the two stallions' lines were merged at the Mezohegyes Stud in Hungary, creating a high-quality, sturdy riding horse.

Breed name: Furioso

Other name: Furioso-North Star, Mezőhegyes Half-bred

Breed purpose: light farm work, riding, driving

Size: 16 hands

Coat color: bay, occasionally black, brown

Place of origin: Hungary

Ancestors: Thoroughbred, Nonius, Norfolk Roadster

Strong ride
Once also popular in neighboring Romania, it is now an endangered breed, with fewer than 500 breeding mares. It is a medium-heavy warmblood with a refined appearance that reflects its Thoroughbred influence.

NONIUS

HUNGARY

The Nonius takes its name from its Anglo-Norman foundation sire, Nonius Senior (born 1810). The stallion was initially not used as a sire as he had what were considered undesirable looks. However, it was found that his offspring did not inherit this problem. They proved to have sturdy constitutions, and in the 19th century, the breed became a popular cavalry horse. Today, the Nonius is often used under harness.

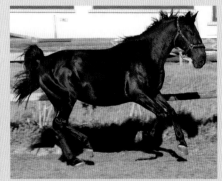

Breed name: Nonius

Other name: n/a

Breed purpose: riding, driving, farm work

Size: 16 hands

Coat color: bay, sometimes black, brown

Pace of origin: Hungary

Ancestors: Anglo-Norman, Arab, Lipizzaner, Holsteiner

Light jumper
Heavier Nonius horses are still used in Hungary for draft work. The Nonius is also often crossed with Thoroughbreds to create a lighter-framed, faster horse.

ORLOV TROTTER

CENTRAL RUSSIA

This breed was founded in the 18th century by Russian Count Alexis Orlov to compete in harness races. All Orlov Trotters are descended from one foundation stallion—an impressive gray Arabian called Smetanka, which Orlov bought in Turkey for a huge price. Faster breeds are often now preferred in races, but the Orlov Trotter's influence is found widely in other Russian breeds.

Breed name: Orlov Trotter	
Other name: n/a	
Breed purpose: harness racing	
Size: 16 hands	
Coat color: gray, dapple gray, black, and bay	
Place of origin: central Russia	
Ancestors: Arab, Mecklenburg, Danish	

Trotting race in Russia

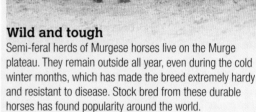

Champion Trotter
The Orlov Trotter has strong legs and a naturally fast trotting gait. It enjoyed its greatest success in harness racing in the 1930s. Since then, other breeds, such as the faster Standardbred, have been preferred.

Dapple gray Orlov trotter

Wild and tough
Semi-feral herds of Murgese horses live on the Murge plateau. They remain outside all year, even during the cold winter months, which has made the breed extremely hardy and resistant to disease. Stock bred from these durable horses has found popularity around the world.

MURGESE

PUGLIA, ITALY

Bred to survive in the dry, occasionally harsh conditions of the Murge plateau in southern Italy, the Murgese is a good all-rounder that can still be seen on small farms doing light draft work. With a strong constitution and hard hooves, it is also popular as a trekking horse.

Breed name: Murgese	**Coat color:** mostly black or blue roan, occasionally gray
Other name: Murge Horse	**Place of origin:** Puglia, Italy
Breed purpose: light farmwork, riding	**Ancestors:** Barb, Arabian
Size: 15–16 hands	

UKRAINIAN RIDING HORSE

UKRAINE

The Soviet Union created this breed after World War II. Ukrainian studs carefully mixed breeds to produce a durable competition horse. The best horses are entered into dressage, show jumping, and eventing competitions, and only those that achieve success are allowed to breed.

Breed name: Ukrainian Riding Horse
Other name: n/a
Breed purpose: riding
Size: 15.1–16 hands
Coat color: bay, chestnut, brown
Place of origin: Ukraine
Ancestors: Trakehner, Nonius, Thoroughbred, Hanoverian

Sure mover
Lightly built but powerful, this confident breed has the courage to tackle most competition challenges. The horses enter training before the age of two and start competing aged three.

KABARDIN

NORTHERN CAUCASUS, RUSSIA

Originally bred 400 years ago in the mountains of the Northern Caucasus, this is a tough and adaptable breed, able to work in cold, dark, or wet conditions. The Kabardin is popular in local sports contests, but does not have the quality to compete at the highest level.

Breed name: Kabardin
Other name: Kabarda
Breed purpose: riding, farmwork
Size: 15–15.2 hands
Coat color: bay, dark bay, black
Place of origin: Northern Caucasus, Russia
Ancestors: Karabakh, Arabian, Turkoman

Mountain herds
Kabardin horses are usually kept in herds in the Caucasus. They move between mountain pastures in the summer and valley pastures in the winter.

Breed name: Don
Other name: Russian Don
Breed purpose: riding, driving
Size: 15.3–16.2 hands
Coat color: chestnut, brown
Place of origin: central Russia
Ancestors: Karabach, Arabian, Thoroughbred, Orlov Trotter

Golden glow
The golden sheen of the coat of a Don is a legacy of its Karabach blood. It also displays the speed and endurance of a Karabach.

DON

CENTRAL RUSSIA

Bred on the grasslands around the Don River in Russia, this horse was the mount of the Russian Cossack cavalry. It was famed for its ability to cover long distances without a break. Today, it is often used to pull the *tachanka*—a carriage pulled by four horses hitched side-by-side.

BUDYONNY

SOUTHERN RUSSIA

Bred by Marshall Budyonny, a famous cavalry commander in the Russian Civil War (1917–1923), this horse was bred to replace horses lost in World War I. It is fast and agile, and has great stamina. No longer needed by the military today, the Budyonny has proved to be a fine competition horse.

Breed name: Budyonny
Other name: Budenny
Breed purpose: riding and driving
Size: 15.1–16.1 hands
Coat color: bay, chestnut, brown
Place of origin: southern Russia
Ancestors: Don, Chernomor, Thoroughbred

Return to the wild
In the 1950s, a group of Budyonny horses were released onto an island in Manych Lake, Russia. They have since thrived on the island, proving that they can survive without human help.

AUSTRALIAN STOCK HORSE

ENDURING ALL-ROUNDER

A versatile horse, the Australian Stock Horse is descended from the very first horses to arrive in Australia. The breed has been adapted to work in the Australian outback and is able to endure the extreme conditions there, including sweltering temperatures and lack of food. This resilient horse is popular for its cattle sense, speed, and bravery, and is dubbed "the breed for every need" in Australia.

Breed name: Australian Stock Horse

Other names: n/a

Breed purpose: competitive disciplines, stock work, hacking, polo

Size: 14–16 hands

Coat color: all colors, commonly bay

Place of origin: Australia

Ancestors: various important breeds, including Thoroughbred, Timor Pony, Arabian, and Welsh Mountain Pony

Heavy lifter
The Australian Stock Horse is a successor of the larger Waler horse —the first breed to be developed in Australia. As many as 120,000 Australian horses, including Stock Horses and Walers, were sent abroad in World War I to transport soldiers, pull carriages, and carry weapons. The Australian Stock Horse has retained the stamina and robust nature of its ancestors.

Surviving the seas
The first British fleet arrived at Botany Bay, Australia, (above) in 1788, in an attempt to further expand the British empire. The explorers brought seven horses, including the English Thoroughbred. The Australian Stock Horse can be traced back to these horses, which had the stamina to endure the long voyage from Europe—only the hardiest survived.

In 2000, **120 Stock Horses** took part in the **Opening Ceremony** of the **Sydney Olympics**.

Fine features
A long, elegant head is typical of this southern hemisphere breed.

Agile build
The athletic body with prominent withers show its Thoroughbred ancestry.

Australian Stock Horse foal running

Clean runner
The thin legs of this foal will develop to become lean but powerful.

Hazardous territory
It is a harsh world in the Australian outback, and the horses brought to the continent were forced to adapt to the challenging environment. Poisonous snakes, severe heat, dehydration, and dangerous predators were just a few of the hazards. Only the strongest horses survived, which is why the Australian Stock Horse has such a resilient nature.

A herd in the outback

Cattle droving in the outback

Drovers on horseback muster cattle at Anna Creek Station, a working 9,300 sq. mile (24,000 sq. km) cattle station in southern Australia. This is the unforgiving landscape of the outback—dry and dusty with temperatures regularly climbing high over 100°F (38°C). Yet this harsh region is where vast herds of cattle graze. Every year, there is a mustering season on remote outback stations, and the cattle are driven to be branded, vet-checked, and ear-marked. Some are exported, while others are returned to the station for breeding.

Willing worker

A cowboy herds his cattle while riding an experienced stock horse. A good stock horse has an instinctive sense of how livestock will react, so they can act with only minimal direction from their riders. This is crucial when the rider needs to concentrate on tasks such as roping cattle. While the cowboy handles his lasso, the horse will know which direction to move in without being given instructions.

STOCK HORSES

Known for their natural "cow sense," stock horses have a talent for working with livestock. They are agile and intelligent, with muscular hindquarters, and respond quickly to moving cattle. As a popular choice for cowboys and cowgirls, stock horses are commonly associated with Western riding. They are seen competing in events such as rodeo, cutting, and roping.

Italian stallion

The cowboys of Tuscany, Italy, known as the *butteri*, are famed for their cattle-herding skills. Their main stock horse is the Maremmano, a rustic breed known for its strength, good nature, and superb cow sense. Today's Maremmano are descended from an outstanding stallion named Fauno, which was born at the Royal Stables in San Rossore, Tuscany, in 1902. The breed takes its name from the Maremma National Park—home to *butteri* to this day.

Maremma National Park

Buttero at work

America's steady steed

Horse-drawn cart from the old West

Compact and muscular, the Quarter Horse is exceptionally fast over short distances, reaching speeds of over 55 mph (88 kph). Early US settlers spotted this talent in the mid-17th century and started competitive racing on horseback. With the stamina to endure long distances too, the Quarter Horse was popular with cowboys, and played an important role in the westward expansion of the American frontier.

Quarter Horse ridden in the Western style

ENTERING NEZ PERCE INDIAN RESERVATION

Sign at the Nez Perce reservation

People of the plateau

The Native American Nez Perce tribe originated from the modern-day Pacific Northwest region of the US. From the 18th century onward, they became famed for their horse riding skills, and developed the Appaloosa breed. They ranged across the rich grasslands of the Columbia River Plateau, hunting buffalo. They were defeated by the US Army in 1877. They are now headquartered in Idaho.

A Nez Perce woman pictured with her horse in 1909

From farm to battlefield

At the end of the 19th century, an Australian stock horse called the Waler earned a reputation as the finest cavalry horse in the world. The Waler was the horse of choice in several divisions of the British Army from 1895, and many horses died on the battlefield during the Second Boer War in South Africa (1899–1902). Today, a memorial stands in ANZAC Square, Brisbane, Australia.

Boer War memorial

Hearst's prized horses

Chosen for its elegance and power, the Morab was first developed in the early 1800s as a cross between Morgan and Arab breeds. Media tycoon William Randolph Hearst (1863–1951), founder of Hearst Communications, further developed the Morab as a workhorse for his Californian ranch in the 1920s. An avid breeder, Hearst is credited with naming the Morab by combining the two breed names.

William Randolph Hearst

A stallion named **Golddust** was one of the earliest **Morab** horses. He sired **302 foals**, and **100 horses** can be **traced** back **to him** today.

Surviving the winter

Most ponies are comforable in cold conditions, their thick coat, mane, and tail protecting them from the harshest winter weather. The Yakutsk pony, for example, grows a coat up to 8 ins (20 cm) long. As long as the coat stays dry, body heat is trapped and keeps the pony warm in temperatures as low as −94°F (−70°C). The tough plants ponies eat are broken down by bacteria in the gut and this too produces heat.

THE SMALLEST IN THE FAMILY

LESS THAN 14.2 HANDS AND BRED FOR SURVIVAL

Ponies are hardy animals that have learned to survive in the harshest of conditions, many on remote northerly islands. They are intelligent, energetic, and sometimes stubborn. Yet they are gentle and steady, and make excellent mounts when children are learning to ride.

Pit ponies living underground

There are over 200 breeds of pony all over the world today, but their ancestors lived wild in northern climates, where survival depended on adapting to the cold weather and sparse vegetation of that habitat. This has produced small, tough animals, used to difficult conditions, that generally live longer than horses.

The essential difference between ponies and horses is one of size. However, although ponies are usually smaller than horses, a few ponies may be more than 14.2 hands, while some horses are smaller than 14.2 hands. There are also differences in bone structure and the shape of the body. Ponies have thicker necks, and smaller heads with broad foreheads. Their bodies are wider in proportion, and their bones are heavier. They have shorter legs, often with feathering on the lower leg, and thicker manes and tails. They are pound for pound stronger than light horses and the Shetland pony is strongest of all. A typical adult pony of any breed can haul around 20 percent of its own body weight.

Over the centuries, these feisty, intelligent animals have been used by people to carry goods, pull carts and carriages, as pit ponies in the mines, as well as for riding. They are surefooted workhorses, with a gentle, steady nature. Easy to care for, ponies need only half the food that a light horse would if it were the same weight.

More recently, breeders have added Arabian and other light horse blood to the pony breeds to develop ponies that are more suitable for riding and competing. Breeds such as the Hackney and Welsh make excellent driving ponies, while Shetlands, Connemaras, and Welsh ponies are very popular for riding, both for pleasure and competitively— Connemaras excel at dressage.

10½P Shetland Pony

Celebration

Portraits, statues, shows, parades—there are many ways in which people honor their local breeds of horses and ponies. This stamp is only one of many that celebrate the Shetland pony.

Riding in the mountains of Mongolia

A pony-drawn cart in the US, c.1904

Single Pony Carriage driving race

Sugar Puff, a 56-year-old **Shetland cross** that died in 2007, holds the record for the **longest-living pony**.

CHINCOTEAGUE

ISLAND PONY

Named after the island of Chincoteague, today these ponies live on the neighboring island of Assateague on the east coast of the US. They are the wild descendants of horses brought to the area in the 17th century. There are two herds on the island, each about 150 strong. The herds are split further into smaller groups called "bands." These bands can often be seen on the beaches around the island.

Breed name: Chincoteague

Other names: Assateague

Breed purpose: farmwork, show, riding

Breed size: 12–13 hands

Coat color: all colors, but mostly pinto with brown or black spots

Place of origin: Assateague Island, United States

Ancestors: unknown

Salty diet

Chincoteagues survive on a diet of coarse grass, mixed with a variety of wild plants, berries, and seaweed. The marshlands of Assateague are salty, and the ponies eat a diet containing dangerously high levels of salt. To deal with this, they drink about twice as much fresh water as domestic horses the same size.

Bloated look
The large amounts of water that the ponies drink can make them appear bloated.

Strong joints
Legs are slender, but the joints are strong and bones are dense.

Misty of Chincoteague

The 1947 novel *Misty of Chincoteague* tells the story of a Chincoteague pony that escapes from Pony Penning Day (see opposite) to live with two orphaned children. The book was inspired by a real-life pony of the same name that author Marguerite Henry had bought as a foal. Henry went on to write three more novels starring Misty, and in 1961, her stories were made into a movie. A statue of Misty stands in downtown Chincoteague (above).

Pony Penning Day

On the last Wednesday of every July, thousands of people gather on Chincoteague Island to watch the annual Pony Penning Day. Most of the ponies on Assateague Island are rounded up by mounted herders and make the short swim to Chincoteague. Here, some of the yearlings are separated from the herd to be auctioned off. The rest of the ponies are given a health check before they are returned to Assateague two days later.

Coat colors

The ponies are of unknown origin, although they may be descended from Moorish horses. Few clues are found in their appearance as they occur in all colors.

Roan

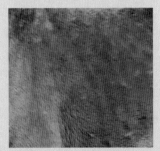
Chestnut

Pinto

Shaggy mane
The pony is protected from cold weather by a thick coat, shaggy mane, and bushy tail.

Spanish legend

According to legend, ponies arrived on Assateague when they swam ashore from a Spanish galleon that ran aground on the island during a storm. The story may have some truth behind it, as a Spanish ship called *La Galga* is known to have shipwrecked on Assateague in 1750.

The ponies swim from Assateague to Chincoteague **during slack tide**—a period after low tide in which **the water is calm**.

AMERICAN SHETLAND PONY

ELEGANT HARNESS PONY

Shetland ponies (see pp.134–135) were first brought to the United States in the late 19th century, and the American Shetland Pony Club was established in 1888. The American Shetland is taller and has a lighter build than its ancestors, but retains the stamina and capacity for hard work, making it a sought-after breed.

Breed name: American Shetland Pony

Other name: n/a

Breed purpose: harness pony, show, riding

Breed size: up to 11.2 hands

Coat color: all solid colors

Country/place of origin: US

Ancestors: Shetland, Hackney, and Welsh Ponies

Fine features
American breeders crossed Shetland ponies with Hackney ponies to produce a sleek show pony that was also capable of pulling carriages. The Hackney influence is clearly seen in the American Shetland's long legs, narrow frame, and attractive, refined head.

Classic or modern
The original Shetland pony is short and stout, with a heavy coat that its ancestors developed living in the chilly Scottish Shetland Isles, UK. The American Shetland has more refined features than pure Shetlands. There are four recognized types, ranging from the Foundation, which is closest to the UK breed, to the high-stepping, lean-bodied modern pony.

Foundation-type American Shetland

Modern-type American Shetland

Top traits
This versatile breed is able to cater for competitive riders, while also being a calm and friendly mount for the less experienced. The breed has an athletic build with a neat head, broad neck, and stout body.

AMERICAN QUARTER PONY

SMALLER VERSION OF THE QUARTER HORSE

Originally bred from horses that failed to reach the minimum height for a Quarter horse, Quarter ponies have many of the physical characteristics of a Quarter horse but are smaller. With strong muscles and a rhythmic gait, this agile pony is used in children's riding competitions.

NORTH AMERICAN SPORT PONY

UNITED STATES

Similar to the American Warmblood, the North American Sport Pony originates from a number of breeds. It was developed as a sports horse and has a good sense of rhythm, which lends itself well to show competitions.

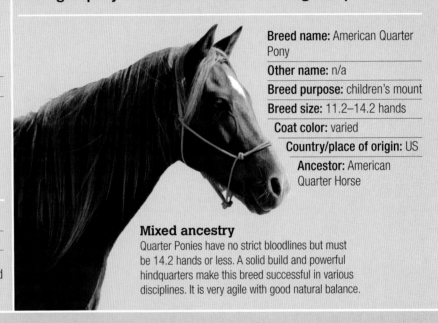

Breed name: American Quarter Pony
Other name: n/a
Breed purpose: children's mount
Breed size: 11.2–14.2 hands
Coat color: varied
Country/place of origin: US
Ancestor: American Quarter Horse

Breed name: North American Sport Pony
Other name: n/a
Breed purpose: riding and competition
Size: 13–14 hands
Coat color: all colors
Place of origin: North America
Ancestors: Quarter horse, Connemara Pony, Arabian, Morgan, Thoroughbred, and Welsh Pony

Mixed ancestry
Quarter Ponies have no strict bloodlines but must be 14.2 hands or less. A solid build and powerful hindquarters make this breed successful in various disciplines. It is very agile with good natural balance.

PONY OF THE AMERICAS

AMERICAN SPOTTED PONY

This striking spotted breed was developed in Iowa, US, and is the ideal mount for children learning to ride. Its foundation stallion was a cross between a Shetland pony and an Appaloosa horse.

An easy ride
Although they are classified as ponies, this breed has many of the physical traits of a small horse, including a narrow body that is easier for young children to ride. This pony is a common choice for young riders competing in Western disciplines.

Breed name: Pony of the Americas
Other names: POA
Breed purpose: children's ride and Western riding
Breed size: 11–14 hands
Coat color: spotted
Place of origin: Iowa, US
Ancestors: Shetland and Appaloosa

ICELANDIC

VIKING STOCK HORSE

This tough pony breed can be traced back to Viking settlers who arrived in Iceland in the 9th century. Although small in size, it is always referred to in Iceland as a horse rather than a pony. Over the centuries, it has developed into a sturdy breed that is well suited to the harsh Icelandic winter where nights are long and very cold. Icelandic horses are often kept in semi-wild herds, and while farmers now rarely use them as working horses, they remain very popular for leisure riding.

Breed name: Icelandic

Other names: n/a

Breed purpose: transport and farm work

Breed size: 13–14 hands

Coat color: wide range, often chestnut

Place of origin: Iceland

Ancestors: Norwegian stock

Pure breed
To maintain the quality of the domestic stock, horses cannot be imported into Iceland from abroad. Icelandics that leave the island are also not allowed to return. Laws preventing imports were first introduced by the Althing, the Icelandic parliament, in 982 CE, which means that the stock has been pure-bred for more than 1,000 years.

Flying pace
The Icelandic Horse has five different gaits. In pacing races, it performs a gait called a *skeio*, or flying pace. Using this fast, smooth pace, the horses can reach speeds of up to 30 mph (48 km/h).

Winter coat
Icelandics grow heavy coats to cope with the bitter winters, when temperatures can fall below −22°F (−30°C).

Thick mane
The mane is typically very thick and coarse.

Running walk
Renowned for its sure-footedness on rough terrain, the Icelandic uses a distinctive four-beat gait known as the *tölt* to cross broken ground. Riders find this "running walk" gait very comfortable.

Horse or pony?
The legs are short and muscular, with relatively short pasterns. This gives a pony-like appearance.

Coat colors

There are around 80,000 horses in Iceland. They come in a wide range of colors, but there are around 15 basic types. Different studs tend to breed animals of one particular color. Many horses are bred for export, particularly to Germany, where there are more than 50,000 Icelandics today.

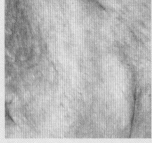

Roan

Gray

Blue roan

Bay

The **oldest** Icelandic ever, **named Tulle**, lived to the ripe old **age of 57**.

Long lives

The Icelandic is renowned as a long-lived breed that develops very few health problems. Both mares and stallions are fit for breeding for up to 25 years, and they can live on for many years after that.

An extraordinary island population

There are an incredible 80,000 Icelandic ponies in a country that has a human population of only 350,000. And they have survived in the challenging habitat that is Iceland for 1,100 years without cross-breeding, making this the purest breed in the world. Carried there on Viking ships, the Althing (the Viking parliament) banned the import of horses in 982 CE, and said that if any left the country they could not return. Today's sure-footed survivors live in a landscape of fjords, volcanoes, giant lava fields, rugged cliffs, and black, sandy beaches.

MOUNTAIN PONIES

SHAPED BY EXTREME CONDITIONS

Conditions on mountainsides can be harsh, and ponies that live there have to be tough to cope. Mountain pony breeds are often small and strong, but they are also usually very friendly and easy to ride, making them a popular choice among families. Many breeds around the world have been experiencing a revival in recent years as people rediscover these lovely animals.

BASHKIR CURLY

NEVADA, US

A tough mountain breed, the Bashkir Curly grows a distinctive thick, curly coat in winter. It also has a thick, dreadlocked mane, curly eyelashes and guard hairs, and even curly hairs inside its ears! Its origins are uncertain, but the Sioux kept curly-haired horses in the early 19th century.

Breed name:	Bashkir Curly
Other name:	Curly
Breed purpose:	riding
Breed size:	average 15 hands
Coat color:	chestnut, bay
Place of origin:	Nevada, US
Ancestors:	unknown, possibly Iberian

Safe curls
The Bashkir Curly's coat is thought to be hypoallergenic. This means that people who are allergic to horses can handle this breed with no adverse reaction.

HUÇUL

CARPATHIAN MOUNTAINS, CENTRAL EUROPE

A strong, sure-footed pony, the Huçul was used as a packhorse to carry people and goods over snowy mountain passes. It was also used by the Austro-Hungarian cavalry. Huçuls are still used for farm work in the Carpathian Mountains today.

Breed name:	Huçul
Other name:	Carpathian
Breed purpose:	packhorse
Size:	13–14 hands
Coat color:	bay, dun, black, or chestnut
Place of origin:	Carpathian Mountains in central Europe
Ancestors:	ancient breed rarely cross-bred

Therapeutic ride
Huçul ponies live across a wide area in the Bieszczady Mountains National Park in Poland. Here they are used in recreational riding (left) and in riding therapy for children with special needs and disabilities.

Summer shine
In winter, the Huçul grows a thick coat to help insulate against the cold mountain conditions. In spring, they shed their winter layers to leave a shiny short-haired summer coat.

HIGHLAND PONY

SCOTTISH HIGHLANDS AND ISLANDS

A hardy breed with an even temperament, this pony makes an excellent children's pony. Originally bred for farm work, the Highland pony is now more commonly seen on pony treks.

Breed name: Highland pony

Other name: n/a

Breed purpose: general workhorse

Size: 13–14.2 hands

Coat color: mostly dun, also gray, brown, or black

Place of origin: Scottish Highlands and Islands

Ancestors: mix, including Percheron, Fell pony

Pedigree pony
Most of today's 5,500 Highland ponies can trace their ancestry back to the stallion Herd Laddie, which was born in 1881.

BOSNIAN MOUNTAIN HORSE

BOSNIA AND HERZEGOVINA

This is the only breed of horse that is native to Bosnia and Herzegovina. Once widely used for transportation, the horse remains the main means of getting around in remote areas.

Alpine horse
The Bosnian Mountain Horse has proved a popular choice among tourists in recent years. They are being used to rediscover remote parts of the Alps, which became accessible after the Bosnian War ended in 1995.

Breed name: Bosnian Mountain Horse

Other name: Bosnian Pony

Breed purpose: transportation, farm work

Size: 13 hands

Coat color: many solid colors

Place of origin: Bosnia and Herzegovina

Ancestors: some Arab lines

FJORD

NORWAY

This strong, stocky breed comes from the mountains of Norway. The Fjord has been used as a farm horse in Norway for hundreds of years. It is still used as a pack pony and under saddle, and is also very popular in long-distance racing.

Breed name: Fjord

Other name: Norwegian Fjord

Breed purpose: farm work

Size: 13–14 hands

Coat color: dun

Place of origin: Norway

Ancestors: ancient pure breed

One color
The Fjord is one of the world's oldest breeds, dating back hundreds of years, but today's horses are all descended from a stallion named Njål, born in 1891, and they are all dun-colored.

ARIÉGEOIS

SOUTHERN FRANCE

This native of the Pyrénées and Ariégeois mountains is well equipped for the cold. However, it suffers in warm weather, when its all-black coat can make it uncomfortably hot. There were only 40 horses registered in the studbook in the 1970s, and it was in danger of extinction, but numbers have since increased.

Breed name: Ariégeois

Other name: Mérens Horse

Breed purpose: farm work and pack horse

Size: 14.1–14.3 hands

Coat color: black

Place of origin: southern France

Ancestors: unknown

Semi-wild herds
Herds of semi-wild Ariégeois follow a regular annual migration pattern. They spend their summers on high mountain pastures and move down to warmer valleys in the winter.

EXMOOR

The ponies that range freely over Exmoor in Devon, England, have remained a very pure breed. The line was nearly killed off entirely during World War II, when the moor was used as an army training ground and the number of ponies dropped as low as 50. Since then, their numbers have risen and there may be up to 300 breeding mares living on the moor.

Breed name: Exmoor	
Other name: n/a	
Breed purpose: draft pony, shows, riding	
Size: 12.2–12.3 hands	
Coat color: bay, brown, or dun	
Place of origin: Exmoor, England	
Ancestors: ancient breed	

An Exmoor breeding mare

Conservation grazers
Exmoor ponies graze on tough plants that most animals will not touch. This allows more delicate plants the space to grow. Herds of Exmoors have been introduced to many heathlands to help conserve the variety of plants there.

Herd on dry heathland

Roaming the moor
These tough ponies have roamed semi-wild on Dartmoor in Devon, England, for more than 3,000 years. They share the moor with cross-breeds known as Dartmoor Hill Ponies.

DARTMOOR

Hardy, beautiful, and with an excellent temperament, the Dartmoor Pony is a highly sought-after breed. Only a few hundred remain on Dartmoor, but the pony is bred in studs around the world, including New Zealand, where herds of ponies help handicapped children.

Breed name: Dartmoor	**Coat color:** mostly bay, black, brown, or gray
Other name: n/a	
Breed purpose: draft pony	**Place of origin:** England
Size: up to 12.2 hands	**Ancestors:** some Arab, Welsh, and Fell blood

CONNEMARA

CONNEMARA, WESTERN IRELAND

The only breed of pony that is native to Ireland, this large pony is prized for its speed, endurance, and jumping ability. It comes from Connemara, a remote region in the far west of Ireland, but has been widely exported, with breeders' societies in 16 different countries. Cross-breeding with Spanish, Arabian, and Barb lines over time has given this pony a mixture of features.

Breed name: Connemara
Other name: n/a
Breed purpose: sports
Size: 12.2–14.2 hands
Coat color: gray, black, bay, brown, or dun; occasionally roan, chestnut, palomino, or cream
Place of origin: Connemara, western Ireland
Ancestors: mixed

Running free
The Connemara retains many of its adaptations to the rugged moorland of western Ireland. However, the introduction of Thoroughbred blood has made the pony taller and faster.

DALES

NORTHERN ENGLAND

Closely related to the Fell, the Dales has a heavier build than its neighbor, and it was widely used as a pit pony in mining in the 18th and 19th centuries. Today, the breed is nearing a crisis, with fewer than 300 breeding mares remaining.

Breed name: Dales
Other name: n/a
Breed purpose: mining, farm work, riding, sport
Size: up to 14.2 hands
Coat color: mostly black, occasionally bay, brown, or gray

Country/place of origin: eastern Pennines, northern England
Ancestors: mixed, including Scottish Galloway, Friesian

Solid bones
The hardy Dales has strong legs, very hard feet, and silky feather in its heels. Its solid bone structure makes this a highly prized breed.

Breed name: Fell
Other name: n/a
Breed purpose: pack horse, riding
Size: up to 14 hands
Coat color: black, brown, bay, or gray
Place of origin: northern England
Ancestors: shared roots with the Dales Pony

Small head
The Fell has a characteristically narrow head leading down to a thin, tapering muzzle.

FELL

NORTHERN ENGLAND

Coming from the Cumbrian moorlands, this strong pony was originally bred as a pack horse. It would travel up to 240 miles (380 km) a week carrying lead, slate, copper, and iron ore. Today, the breed is highly sought after for leisure riding, competitions, and trekking. It is noted for its fast trot.

NEW FOREST

NEW FOREST, ENGLAND

Local people have had the right to graze their ponies in the New Forest for nearly 1,000 years. In the 1940s, there were fewer than 600 ponies, but breeding programmes have seen their numbers increase greatly, and thousands now live in small, semi-wild herds throughout the forest.

Breed name: New Forest
Other name: n/a
Breed purpose: mining, grazing, riding
Size: up to 14.2 hands

Coat color: all except piebald, skewbald, spotted, or blue-eyed cream
Place of origin: England
Ancestors: mixed including Celtic

Forest life
The ponies are rounded up twice a year for health checks, during which some are selected for sale. This is done to control their numbers.

Central heating

Mountain ponies have large digestive systems that are adapted to getting the most out of heathland plants that are low in nutrients. The process of digesting large quantities of these coarse plants in their large guts produces heat as the food is broken down. This provides the ponies with a source of internal warmth in the depths of a freezing winter.

BUILT TO SURVIVE

Mountain and moorland ponies are a group of tough breeds, and many of them still live semi-wild on high moors and heathland. Here, winter temperatures can fall well below freezing and there is little shelter from storms and high winds. Their stocky bodies are well suited to life in these remote places, and they are able to thrive by eating plants that other horse breeds would struggle to survive on.

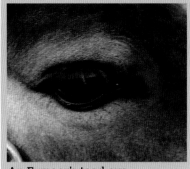
An Exmoor's toad eye

Winter coats
Thick, double-layered coats keep Exmoors warm in winter. The fine undercoat forms a layer of insulation next to the skin. The outer hairs are coarse and greasy, and create a waterproof outer layer. This coat is so effective at keeping in heat that snow can collect on the ponies without melting. The ponies have to shake the snow off their backs from time to time.

Snow collecting on ponies in the Welsh hills

Toad eyes
Some mountain breeds such as the Exmoor have fleshy "toad eyes." The extra rim of flesh helps to protect the eyes from the rain, but it can lead to problems later on. When they get older, pure-bred Exmoor ponies are likely to get cataracts, a condition where the eye lens clouds over, damaging sight.

Conserving their habitat
Mountain ponies play an important role in the conservation of heathlands. Their grazing stops shrubs from taking over the land. They also spread seeds in their droppings, encouraging a wide variety of plants. In areas that have lots of wildfires, such as the heathlands of Galicia in Spain, the grazing of these ponies controls the woody undergrowth, reducing the risk of fire.

A pit pony in Nova Scotia, Canada

Pit ponies
From the 18th century to the mid-20th century, ponies were put to work in mines throughout Europe, hauling loads from the coalface to the surface. Mountain ponies such as Shetlands were often preferred due to their small size and powerful build. These ponies would be kept underground, and would rarely come to the surface. In the US, mules were more commonly used.

Welsh Hill ponies on heathland

Ice tail
The tail of the Exmoor contains a fan of short hairs at the top. These turn the tail into a chute, down which snow and rain can run off the body. The tail hair sheds in the summer, and grows again each fall.

An Exmoor pony showing its lighter, summer tail

SHETLAND

BRED FOR STRENGTH

This exceptionally strong pony comes from the windswept Shetland Islands, which lie north of mainland Scotland. In the 19th century, the tough Shetland breed was used as a pit pony, and an even stronger, heavier type was developed to pull larger, heavier loads. Some were even sent to the US to work in mines there. Today, smaller versions of the Shetland are popular as children's mounts.

Breed name: Shetland

Other names: n/a

Breed purpose: farm work, riding

Breed size: up to 10.2 hands

Coat color: any except spotted

Place of origin: Scotland

Ancestors: unknown, but has links to the Icelandic Horse

Bronze Age pony
Ponies have lived in the Shetland Islands since the Bronze Age. It is thought that the native ponies were crossed with ponies brought by Viking invaders in the 9th century CE. They were used by farmers to carry peat and to pull carts and plows.

Protecting the ponies
Ponies and their foals grazing on the heathery hills are a common sight as you travel around the Shetland Islands. The ponies roam free, but they are all owned by local crofters (farmers), who keep a close eye on their valuable little companions.

For **its size**, the Shetland may be **the strongest** of all horse and pony breeds, able to pull **twice its own weight**.

Racing Shetlands
Despite their small size, Shetlands are raced against each other in a number of events, including harness racing, driving, and steeplechase (racing over jumps). There is even a Shetland Pony Grand National, named after the famous horse race that is held at Aintree, Liverpool, UK, every year.

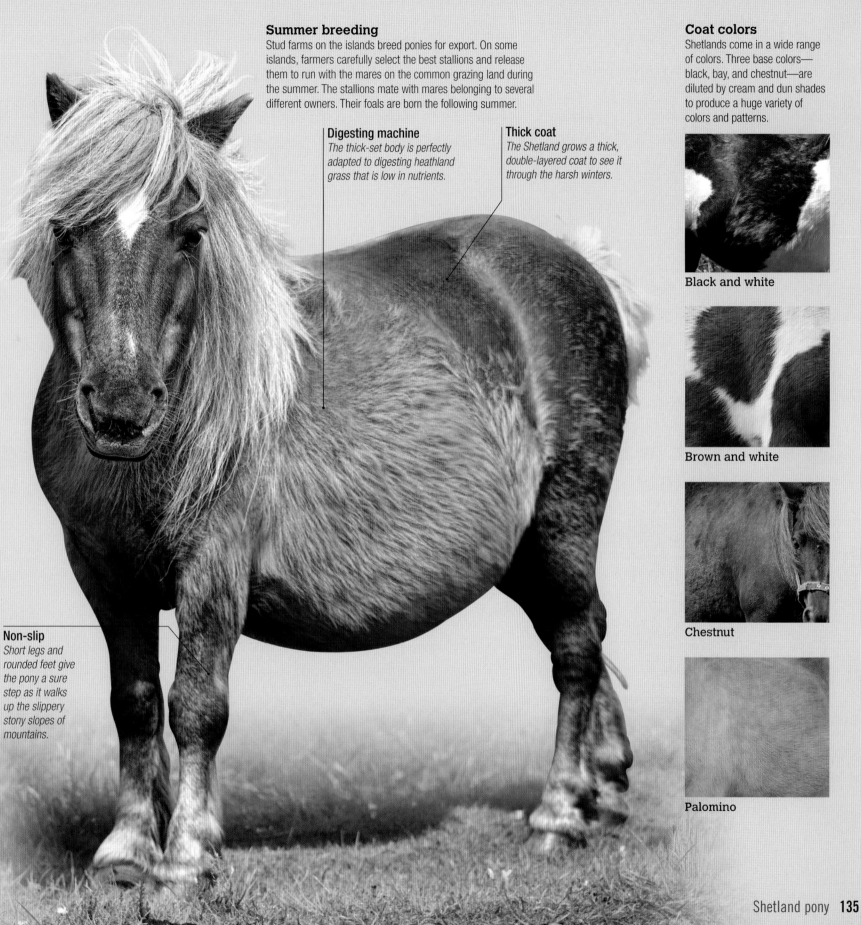

Summer breeding

Stud farms on the islands breed ponies for export. On some islands, farmers carefully select the best stallions and release them to run with the mares on the common grazing land during the summer. The stallions mate with mares belonging to several different owners. Their foals are born the following summer.

Digesting machine
The thick-set body is perfectly adapted to digesting heathland grass that is low in nutrients.

Thick coat
The Shetland grows a thick, double-layered coat to see it through the harsh winters.

Non-slip
Short legs and rounded feet give the pony a sure step as it walks up the slippery stony slopes of mountains.

Coat colors

Shetlands come in a wide range of colors. Three base colors—black, bay, and chestnut—are diluted by cream and dun shades to produce a huge variety of colors and patterns.

Black and white

Brown and white

Chestnut

Palomino

WILD ISLAND PONIES

SEMI-WILD BREEDS

Life on an island can be tough! Wild and semi-wild herds of ponies living on islands across the world have had to adapt over time to hard living conditions and they have done this in a multitude of ways. And people have worked with these herds, first to ride or as farm horses, but in recent years increasingly to conserve their existence and unique way of life.

ERISKAY

WESTERN ISLES, SCOTLAND

A distinctive breed, with ancient Celtic and Norse connections, this pony was originally used for riding and to carry peat and seaweed for residents of the isle. The breed became almost extinct in the 1970s, with only 21 animals remaining. Today, they live free on the heathland around the Scottish Isles.

Breed name: Eriskay

Other name: n/a

Breed purpose: riding, pack pony

Size: 12–13.2 hands

Coat color: usually gray, but can be black or bay

Place of origin: outer Hebrides, Scotland

Ancestors: original native ponies, Icelandic horse, Faroe pony, Arab, Clydesdale, Norwegian Fjord

Crofter's pony

The Eriskay's dense, waterproof coat protects it from the wet and windy conditions. The pony is immensely strong and has adapted to survive on very poor grazing land, often supplementing the diet with salty seaweed. It is an excellent riding pony.

A remote farm on Eriskay

Roaming the heathland

Small breed
This tiny pony is friendly and even-tempered. Its short legs support a sturdy, well-built frame. The ancestor of this pony may have pulled Alexander the Great's chariot.

Breed name: Skyros	
Other name: Skyrian pony	
Breed purpose: pack animal	
Size: 9.1–11 hands	
Coat color: mainly bay; brown, chestnut, gray, dun	
Place of origin: Greece	
Ancestors: unknown	

SKYROS
SKYROS, GREECE

Native to Greece, this rare breed is only found in the wild on Skyros in the Aegean Sea, and is a protected species. A pony with ancient origins, it is very like the horses depicted on the Parthenon temple in Athens, that dates from 438 BCE.

BATAK
CENTRAL SUMATRA, INDONESIA

Bred by the people with whom it shares its name, this slender pony is hardy and tough, and has a fast pace. Today used mostly for riding, the pony has long been a central part of everyday life on Sumatra.

Breed name: Batak	**Coat color:** wide range
Other name: Deli pony	**Place of origin:** Sumatra, Indonesia
Breed purpose: riding, racing, packhorses	**Ancestors:** Mongolian pony, Arabian
Size: 12.2 hands	

JAVA
JAVA, INDONESIA

During the 17th century, the Dutch East India Company established a trading post for spices on the island of Java. They introduced oriental horses and bred them with native horses to produce the Java pony to transport goods.

Breed name: Java	
Other name: Kuningan pony	
Breed purpose: packhorse and riding	
Size: 11–12 hands	
Coat color: all colors	
Place of origin: Indonesia	
Ancestors: Mongolian pony, Arabian, Barb	

Endurance
The Java is larger and stronger than other Indonesian breeds. It has muscular legs, a long back, and a high-set tail that probably comes from its Arabian ancestors. It has developed a high resistance to heat, and has great stamina.

PADANG
SUMATRA, INDONESIA

The Dutch East India Company bred the Padang from the local pony, the Preanger, by importing ponies from Batak. Later cross-breeding has produced a strong pony that hardly sweats when working in the hottest weather.

Breed name: Padang	
Other name: n/a	
Breed purpose: riding, farm work, cart pony	
Size: 11.2–12.2 hands	
Coat color: wide range	
Place of origin: Indonesia	
Ancestors: Preanger, Batak, Arab	

Tourist attraction
Padangs have small heads, short, muscular necks, and a strong back. They are also even-tempered and have good endurance, which makes them useful for many different tasks. Today, the ponies are a common sight on the island pulling colorful taxi carts.

DÜLMEN

GERMANY

The only pony breed native to Germany, there is just one wild herd of Dülmen ponies left today, living on the estate of the Duke of Croy. They are rounded up each May, when the foals are separated to be sold. The mares and one or two stallions are returned to the estate.

Breed name: Dülmen

Other name: n/a

Breed purpose: farm work, riding

Size: 12–13 hands

Coat color: mostly dun, bay, black, or chestnut

Place of origin: Westphalia, Germany

Ancestors: believed to have developed from primitive types

Fine form
The Dülmen has sloping hindquarters, a short neck, and small ears. The head is medium-sized with sharp, angular features.

SORRAIA

PORTUGAL

The ancestors of the Sorraia, a small pony-like horse, lived in the Sorraia Basin between the rivers Sor and Raia. It was once widespread, but just two herds remain today—one in Portugal and another in Germany. The Sorraia is very hardy and can survive on sparse vegetation.

Breed name: Sorraia

Other name: n/a

Breed purpose: ranch work

Breed size: 14–14.2 hands

Coat color: dun-gray

Place of origin: Portugal

Ancestors: Andalusian and Lusitano

Endangered breed
The Sorraira is under threat of extinction, with fewer than 80 breeding mares remaining. However, it has won many admirers around the world, and efforts are being made to boost its numbers. It is valued as a healthy breed with an independent nature, which makes it very easy to keep.

FRENCH SADDLE

FRANCE

This pony was developed in the 1970s for children to ride in competition. It has the thick-set frame of a pony but the athletic ability of a horse, and it is equally adept at dressage, show jumping, and eventing.

Breed name: French Saddle Pony

Other name: Poney Français de Selle

Breed purpose: equestrian sports

Size: 12.2–14.2 hands

Coat color: all

Place of origin: France

Ancestors: various

Small head
There are significant differences between various bloodlines of this pony. However, it generally has a small, well-formed head with a straight profile.

Mountain pony
This hardy pony has a muscular appearance and strong legs, which it needs to survive in the rough, mountainous terrain of the Apennines. It is well suited to work under harness and competes in races in Italy.

BARDIGIANO

APENNINE MOUNTAINS, ITALY

In the early 20th century, Bardigianos were used by the Italian military to produce mules, and the breed nearly died out. Breeding efforts using the few pure breeds left in the high mountains have seen a recent revival.

Breed name: Bardigiano

Other name: Bardi Horse

Breed purpose: farm work and riding

Size: 13.1–14.1 hands

Coat color: dark bay

Place of origin: Italy

Ancestors: mixture of ancient breeds from Spain, Iran, and Noricum (Roman Austria)

LANDAIS

LANDES, FRANCE

Landais ponies are well-known for their endurance. In 1976, a Landais called Dragon was taken on a 1,800-mile (2,900-km) journey around France in just 100 days. The pony is also an excellent trotter, and a Landais holds the trotting record for the 62-mile (100-km) run between Paris and Chartres.

Breed name: Landais

Other name: Barthais

Breed purpose: riding and driving

Size: 11.1–13 hands

Coat color: bay, brown, chestnut, and black

Place of origin: Landes, France

Ancestors: ancient breed mixed with Arab and Welsh blood

Stud program
Landais numbers are critically low, with just around 50 births per year. French national studs have prioritized the breeding of Landais ponies to ensure their survival.

PINDOS

NORTHERN GREECE

This tough little pony's body and character have been formed by the harsh conditions of the Pindus Mountains. The breed is believed to be descendants of the ancient Thessalian horses used by Alexander the Great (*see pp.40–41*). These ponies are also used for breeding mules.

Breed name: Pindos

Other name: Thessalonian

Breed purpose: riding and draft

Size: 11.1–12.1 hands

Coat color: bay, brown, and gray

Place of origin: northern Greece

Ancestors: various crossbreeding of uncertain origin

Shepherd's mount
With poor soil and little vegetation, the mountains of Greece have shaped a small, sure-footed breed. It is still ridden by shepherds in remote mountain areas.

An ancient breed

On a mountaintop in the Pyrénées, Pottoks drink from a tarn—the name Pottok is the local word for "little horse." Some people believe that this ancient breed can be traced to prehistoric times, 40,000 years ago. Small herds of these semi-feral ponies still range the hills of the Basque country between France and Spain foraging for hay and grass. They have large heads, long bodies, and short, slim legs, and their heavy winter fur grows up to 4 ins (10 cm) in length. In the past, they have been used to carry goods, especially by smugglers.

SUMBA

SUMBA, INDONESIA

This pony takes its name from the island of Sumba, but it is now found on the other islands of Indonesia. It is immensely strong and is still used as the main form of transportation in mountainous areas. Its cooperative, quiet nature makes it an ideal riding horse.

Breed name: Sumba	**Coat color:** any solid color
Other name: n/a	**Place of origin:** Indonesia
Breed purpose: riding, traditional sports	**Ancestors:** central Asian ponies
Size: 12.2 hands	

Dances and games
The Sumba pony is ridden in many traditional Indonesian dances. It is also the mount for competitors in a spear-throwing contest called the *Pasola*, which is held each year at the start of the rice-planting season.

Dressed up for a traditional dance called *sequunt*

Men taking part in the *Pasola*

Surviving the cold
Hokkaido ponies thrive in their northerly home, where temperatures fall well below freezing for several months a year. These tough ponies have a well-earned reputation for hardiness and strength.

HOKKAIDO

HOKKAIDO, JAPAN

Ponies were introduced to the Japanese island of Hokkaido in the 15th century by settlers who came from nearby Honshu. They were used widely in agriculture and later as pit ponies. Today, the majority of the 3,000 ponies left range freely across the island, where they are rounded up once a year for a health check.

Breed name: Hokkaido	**Coat color:** roan and other solid colors
Other name: Dosanko	
Breed purpose: farming and mining	**Place of origin:** Japan
Size: 12.3–13.1 hands	**Ancestors:** ancient stock mixed with Mongolian

TOKARA

KYUSHU, JAPAN

Native to the Tokara Islands at the western tip of Kyushu, this pony was once widely used on sugar cane plantations. However, its numbers declined sharply from the 1960s as farming became mechanized. Due to its small size, it is rarely used for riding and this has reduced demand further.

Breed name: Tokara	
Other name: Kagoshima	
Breed purpose: farm work	
Size: up to 13 hands	
Coat color: bay, brown, chestnut, or roan	
Place of origin: Japan	
Ancestors: horses brought from Korea and Mongolia in the 3rd century CE	

Life at the zoo
Three Tokara mares are kept at Hirakawa Zoo in Kagoshima. The breed has also been reintroduced to the islands, where only one remained in 1974. However, with only about 100 individuals left, this small pony's future is uncertain.

KISO

CENTRAL HONSHU, JAPAN

Once widespread across the Japanese island of Honshu, the Kiso fell out of favor at the start of the 20th century, when the Japanese Army replaced the pony with larger horses. By the end of World War II, just one breeding stallion remained, and his son, Daisan-haruyama, born in 1951, is the foundation stallion of all today's ponies. Their numbers remain very low at perhaps a few hundred.

Breed name: Kiso	
Other name: n/a	
Breed purpose: military horse	
Size: 13 hands	
Coat color: bay, brown, chestnut, and roan	
Place of origin: Japan	
Ancestors: stock from mainland Asia	

Breeding center
The main center for breeding Kiso ponies is the *Kiso Uma no Sato*, or Kiso Horse Land, below Mount Kiso Ontake in central Honshu. The ponies are bred by two separate stables, and graze on the wide pastures to the east of the mountain.

AUSTRALIAN

AUSTRALIA

Horses were introduced to Australia when the first European settlers arrived in 1788. The Australian has a varied bloodline that includes a Hungarian stallion that arrived in the 19th century with a traveling circus. This mixture of ancestors has produced an attractive pony that is ideal for show competitions, including dressage, eventing, show jumping, and gymkhanas.

Breed name: Australian	**Coat color:** any solid color, but mostly gray
Other name: n/a	**Place of origin:** Australia
Breed purpose: children's mount	**Ancestors:** Welsh, Exmoor, Welsh Cob, Hungarian
Size: 12–14 hands	

Competition pony
With its long stride, smooth action, and small size, the Australian is an ideal mount for children. It is regularly seen at show jumping events.

FALABELLA

MINIATURE HORSE OF THE GRASSLANDS

Although it is the size of a very small pony, the Falabella is classified as a miniature horse. This tiny breed was first developed in Argentina in the mid-19th century by Irishman Patrick Newtall. By only allowing his smallest horses to breed, Newtall developed a miniature herd, which he later passed on to his son-in-law Juan Falabella. The Falabella family further developed the breed by introducing bloodlines from Shetland ponies, small Thoroughbreds, and others.

Breed name: Falabella

Other names: n/a

Breed purpose: children's horse, showhorse

Size: up to 8 hands

Coat color: all colors and patterns

Place of origin: Argentina

Ancestors: local breeds including Criollo, Thoroughbred, Shetland, and other small horses

Exporting the breed

The Falabella family expanded its business to the United States in the 1960s. Two major producers of Falabellas have been the original Argentinian farm, and a stud in South Carolina. Breeders continue to strive for ever-smaller but perfectly formed horses.

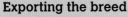

Fine head of hair
The variety of bloodlines used to create the Falabella have produced a horse with a thick, flowing mane.

Large head
The head is often a little larger in proportion to the rest of its body than that of a full-sized horse.

Weak legs
Falabella horses often have weak legs that sometimes cause them to walk with a crooked action.

Cup-shaped hooves
The small, sharp hooves are quite narrow and oval in shape.

Spotted coats

Falabella breeders have two main aims. The first is to produce the smallest horses possible. The second is to expand the range of coat colors available. One of the first Falabellas exported to the US was a black leopard Appaloosa stallion named Chianti, whose lines have expanded the breed to include spotted horses.

Perfectly formed

The Falabella's tiny size and weak legs mean that these miniature horses can only be ridden by small children. Even so, they are good-tempered and very easy to train, making them ideal as show horses. They can also be used to pull miniature carriages.

Coat colors

The Falabella family crossed many different breeds to produce miniature horses in a wide range of colors. Crosses with Criollos and other breeds with Pinto or Appaloosa coats have produced many different patterns.

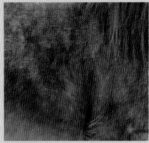

Chestnut

Gray

Brown and white

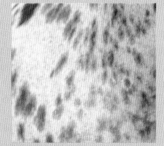

Appaloosa

Attractive feature

A long, bushy tail is highly prized in a Falabella.

Staying slim

To keep trim, the horses must not eat too much—it is easy to overfeed miniature horses.

Small is beautiful

A young Falabella with attractive features, such as a thick and flowing mane and tail, can sell for tens of thousands of dollars. The smaller the horse is, the more it is likely to cost. Falabellas are worth a lot more than most other miniature horses, and only animals descended from Patrick Newtall's original herd qualify for the breed. Each new foal is issued with a certificate to confirm its prestigious ancestry.

Small but perfectly shaped

When breeding miniatures, some people use strict rules, limiting the horses to 8.5 hands or even less. Their aim is to produce the perfect miniature horse and they believe that the smaller the horse, the better. The goal is to breed tiny horses that, if all the references to size were removed, would appear to be identical to full-sized light breeds.

MINIATURE HORSES

Miniature horses are defined as horses that stand less than 9.5 hands (38 inches/96.5 cm) tall at the withers, although some people only accept a maximum height of 8.5 hands (34 inches/ 86 cm). These tiny horses are produced by breeding only the smallest animals in a herd, steadily reducing the height of the animals over several generations.

Guide horse
Miniature horses are often trained as guide horses for the visually impaired. This horse, named Scout, is leading his owner through an airport. He is wearing sneakers to protect him from sharp objects on the ground. The sneakers also help his hooves to grip on slippery indoor surfaces.

Soft sneaker

Miniature horse at a petting zoo

Horse or pony?
Although miniature horses are generally smaller than most ponies, they often retain the slim bodies and legs of horses. For this reason, some people argue that thick-set but short ponies, such as the Shetland, are not miniature horses. Other people maintain that size is all that matters.

Guide horse

Thumbelina, a miniature **brown mare** from St. Louis, Missouri, is the world's **smallest living horse**, at just **17.5 inches (44.5 cm)**.

Perfect pets
Miniature horses were first bred in Europe in the 17th century. At first, tiny breeds were developed as pets for the very rich. Later, they were put to work in mines. In recent years, their popularity as pets has returned. They can be ridden by very small children, and they can also be used to pull carriages.

Pulling carriages in Ontario, Canada

Tacked-up miniature with young rider

Health problems
The intensive breeding that is needed to produce miniature horses leaves them vulnerable to various weaknesses. They have small internal organs, and overwork can put stresses on their hearts. They can also be prone to liver and breathing difficulties. Despite these problems, miniature horses often have a longer lifespan than larger horses, living up to 35 years.

American miniature mare and foal

HEAVY

HORSES

Pulling power

Heavy horses can reach weights of 2,600 lbs (1,180 kg) and one heavy horse can pull a load of up to 8,000 lbs (3,630 kg), But two of these horses that are used to working together can pull three times as much— 24,000 lbs (10,890 kg)! There are many horse pulling competitions around the world in which the heavy horses pull heavier and heavier weights until one team wins. Blinders stop them from being distracted.

THE WORKING HORSES

AT LEAST 16 HANDS AND BRED FOR STRENGTH

Heavy horses, also known as coldbloods or draft horses, are gentle giants. They are tall, muscular, and patient, and their size and strength has been very useful over time, whether to carry knights in heavy armor into battle, or pull weighty plows across muddy fields.

18th-century etching of a draft horse

These horses are called coldbloods because of their temperament. They are calm by nature and respond well to commands. They are descended from ancient European horses used for farming and bred for heavy labor. Today there are more than two dozen breeds across the world.

These are the largest and tallest of all the horses, and most heavy horses share particular characteristics. They have great stamina, and are heavy-boned with strong shoulders, which comes in useful when pulling large loads. They usually have thick manes, tails, and coats because they came from frosty northern regions, unlike the hotbloods, most of which were bred in hot and dry desert areas. Most heavy horses have silky hair, known as "feathers," over the lower half of their legs, sometimes covering their hooves. And they have broad feet that give

Horseshoes
People began to protect horses' feet almost as soon as they began to use them for work. During the Crusades, iron horseshoes were even accepted in the place of money to pay taxes.

them better traction (pulling force) on uneven ground such as an unplowed field or unmade road.

Although they do share certain traits, there are a wide variety of heavy horses. They include well-known breeds such as Percheron, Icelandic, Clydesdale, and Shire. These horses were for hundreds of years sturdy and calm on the field of battle, or a vital part of the workforce for farming and industry in many countries. However, in the 20th century, tractors and four-wheeled vehicles took over most of their working roles.

Today, heavy horses are still used on some farms, and for logging. They are also the most popular breeds in competitions for driving or cart racing, as well as in the show ring. Friesian heavy horses have more of a warmblood temperament so are more suited to the dressage ring. Some are also a popular choice for trail riding.

Hauling logs in Flagstaff, Arizona

An Amish farmer and his team of horses

A 17-year old **Belgian Draft** from Wisconsin, **Big Jake**, is the world's **tallest horse** at **20 hands 2.75 ins**.

Feathered legs of Clydesdale horses

Large eyes
The large eyes are bright, well set, and expressive.

Powerful back
The Shire's back is short, tough and very muscular.

Hindquarters
These are long and sweeping, wide, and strong.

Head room
The head is long and lean, and the nose has thin, wide nostrils.

Glossy mane
The fine mane is straight and silky, but not very long.

Straight legs
The upper part of the legs above the knee is straight.

Hard-working
The solid legs are broad and well-muscled, allowing the horse to pull heavy loads.

Good support
The wide hooves are at the base of deep and wide feathered feet.

Power-packed
Shire horses are powerhouses, and in their time have pulled the heaviest plows, barges, buses, carriages, and carts. Once these gentle giants were everywhere, in cities and towns as well as in the country. Today, they still do some agricultural work, but are more likely to be seen in horse shows and as riding horses.

SHIRE

TRADITIONAL DRAFT HORSE

Probably the largest and strongest breed in the world, the Shire is famous as a gentle giant with a calm, easy-going temperament. Bred as a draft horse, it is capable of pulling enormous weights—in 1924, a pair of Shires pulled a load of 50 tons, which was measured on a dynamometer at the British Empire Exhibition at Wembley, London. The breed's foundation stallion, the Packington Blind Horse, sired foals between 1755 and 1770.

Breed name: Shire

Other name: n/a

Breed purpose: draft horse

Breed size: 17–18 hands

Coat color: black, gray, brown, or bay

Place of origin: England

Ancestors: possibly English Great Horses, Flemish, Friesian

Falling numbers
The number of Shires employed in draft work has plummeted, and their population has fallen from millions at their peak to fewer than 1,500 worldwide, more rare than the giant panda.

The **largest recorded** horse in history was a **Shire** named **Mammoth**, which stood **21.2 hands** at the withers.

Straight path
Shires are bred to be efficient movers. They keep their hocks close together to provide force in a straight line in the direction of movement. Over a long day's work pulling a plow or a heavy cart, this efficiency saves energy and allows the horse to work longer without getting tired.

Park life
In recent years, Shire horses have returned to the countryside of England, thanks to a breeding program called Operation Centaur. The horses, such as this pair in Devon (above), cause less damage to plants than heavier machinery, and they also make much less noise.

Blinder view
Blinders stop a horse from seeing to the side, so they stay on course.

Highly decorated
For shows, it is traditional for owners to braid the mane and tail of their Shires, and decorate the horse with ribbons and bows. They may also add colorful ornaments called "*flights*" (right) to the mane.

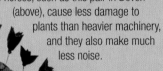
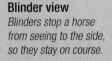

Coat colors
Black, brown, bay, or gray is allowed by the breed registry but not roan or chestnut (although chestnut is allowed in the US). White body patches are also not allowed in purebreds.

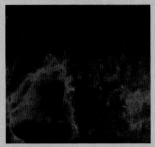
Black

Bay

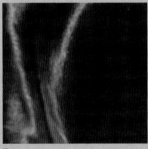
Brown

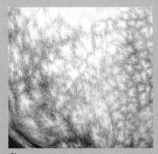
Gray

Horses at Hollesley Bay, the oldest breeding stud

SUFFOLK PUNCH

SUFFOLK, ENGLAND

While the origins of the breed are uncertain, all Suffolks trace their ancestry to a foundation stallion born in 1768. The breed is shorter but more solidly built than other British draft horses, making it ideal for farm and forestry work. You can enjoy this classic breed at country fairs in Suffolk, where the horses are challenged to traditional strength tests. They drop to their knees as they pull on heavy loads such as fallen trees.

Breed name: Suffolk Punch

Other name: Suffolk Horse, Suffolk Sorrel

Breed purpose: draft horse, agriculture

Size: 16–16.3 hands

Coat color: seven different shades of chestnut

Place of origin: Suffolk, England

Ancestors: uncertain

Braiding to compete in a decorated harness event

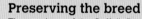

Preserving the breed
The numbers of the Suffolk Punch have declined in recent years with fewer than 300 breeding mares. The Suffolk Punch Trust works to reverse this trend by organizing shows and events that celebrate this ancient breed. The annual Suffolk Punch Spectacular features competitions including decorated harness, braiding, and gymkhana.

Traveling the world
The Suffolk Punch has been a popular horse for crossbreeding, producing a heavier draft horse. The breed contributed to the creation of the Jutland breed in Denmark and the Vladimir Heavy Draft horse in Russia. In the 20th century, it was exported to Pakistan and crossed with native horses to create a breed for military work.

CLYDESDALE

CLYDE VALLEY, SCOTLAND

This elegant breed was established in the 18th century by the Duke of Hamilton, who raised horses on his estate in the lowlands of Scotland. In the late 19th and early 20th centuries, the horse was exported from its native Scotland as far afield as Japan, the United States, and Australia to become one of the most successful heavy breeds in the world. In Australia, the Clydesdale's popularity and importance led to it being dubbed "the breed that built Australia."

Breed name: Clydesdale

Other name: n/a

Breed purpose: draft, show, tourism

Size: 16.2–18 hands

Coat color: mostly bay, brown, black, or chestnut, also gray and roan

Place of origin: Clydesdale, Scotland

Ancestors: Flemish horses

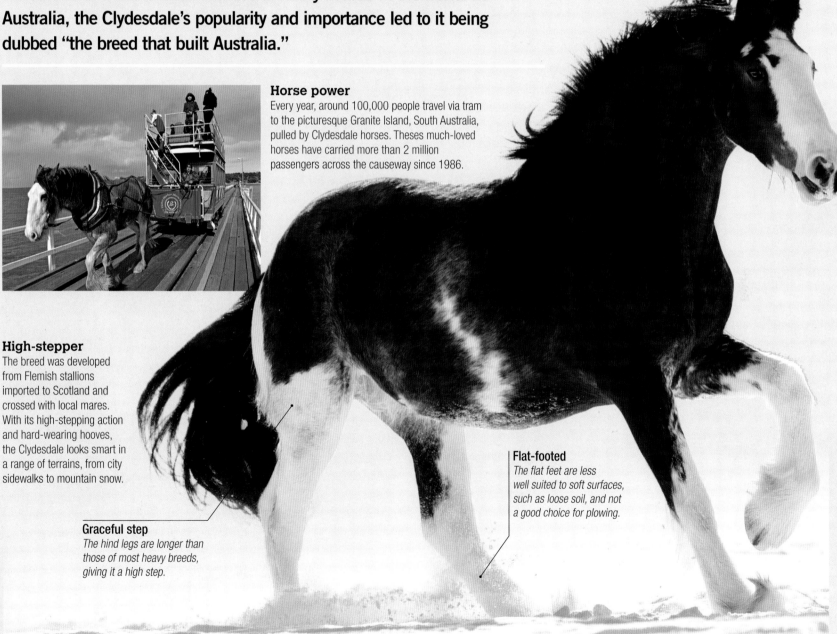

Horse power
Every year, around 100,000 people travel via tram to the picturesque Granite Island, South Australia, pulled by Clydesdale horses. Theses much-loved horses have carried more than 2 million passengers across the causeway since 1986.

High-stepper
The breed was developed from Flemish stallions imported to Scotland and crossed with local mares. With its high-stepping action and hard-wearing hooves, the Clydesdale looks smart in a range of terrains, from city sidewalks to mountain snow.

Graceful step
The hind legs are longer than those of most heavy breeds, giving it a high step.

Flat-footed
The flat feet are less well suited to soft surfaces, such as loose soil, and not a good choice for plowing.

Pulling their weight and more

Clydesdales are among the tallest of the breeds, and their height is matched by their weight, which at 1,600 lbs (726 kg) is about the same as a Volkswagen Beetle. They are the ultimate draft horses, hauling the heaviest farm machinery, logs, freight, and milk wagons. They are also the perfect horses at public events, with their distinctive white facial markings, white lower legs with feathering, and proud, high-stepping walk. Here, a team of Clydesdales strut their stuff at a St Patrick's Day parade in Atlanta, Georgia.

Medieval battle

This painting shows close-quarter fighting in the medieval Battle of Mühldorf in 1322, in which a Bavarian army defeated Austrian forces in Bavaria, southern Germany. Most of the soldiers fought on horseback, supported by mercenary soldiers, including lines of mounted archers. Each individual knight was responsible for providing his own horse, armor, and weaponry. The knights would practice the horsemanship skills needed on the battlefield in jousting tournaments.

HORSES AT WAR

Horses were a crucial part of warfare for more than 5,000 years. As horsemanship improved, the speed and mobility of mounted cavalry became crucial to success on the battlefield. By the 18th century, horses were also needed to transport the troops and supplies of large armies. In the 20th century, cavalry units were largely replaced by tanks, as mounted soldiers were no longer a match for heavy guns and artillery.

East Asian conquerors
At the start of the 13th century CE, a great military leader from Mongolia named Genghis Khan established a huge empire. At its peak, the Mongolian Empire reached all the way from Korea in the east to Hungary in the west. Every Mongol soldier was a skilled horseman, keeping up to six horses and riding a different one each day to keep them all fresh.

Genghis Khan on horseback

Great Horses
In medieval Europe, mounted knights were the elite forces of an army. The most highly prized—and expensive—warhorses were known as *destriers*. Also called Great Horses, these were large, strong stallions, able to carry the weight of a knight in full armor. Hot-blooded destriers were preferred, and in the heat of battle, the horses would often be seen fighting one another.

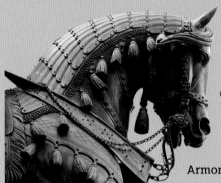

Armored destrier

Comanche warriors

Plains warriors
Between the 1850s and 1870s, a series of conflicts took place on the Great Plains of North America between Native Americans and the United States. During the wars, the Comanche of the southern plains were particularly feared for their horsemanship. Trained from an early age to bring down buffalo, mounted Comanche warriors were highly accurate and fast archers.

End of the cavalry
At the start of World War I in 1914, a British cavalry charge at Mons in Belgium failed when the horses were cut down by German machine-gun fire. It quickly became clear that mounted attacks were no longer an effective tactic. However, horses continued to play a central role at the front, hauling supplies and artillery across rough terrain. By the end of the war in 1918, more than 8 million horses had been killed in action.

British cavalry resting their horses in France

"**Conquering** the world **on horseback** is **easy.**" Genghis Khan

Sergeant Reckless
During the Korean War (1950–1953), the US Army used horses to carry supplies and to rescue wounded soldiers. One horse called Reckless was famed for her bravery under fire, and was awarded the rank of staff sergeant. On one day in March 1953, Sergeant Reckless made 51 trips to the front line to deliver ammunition, all undertaken on her own. She was trained to lie down when under fire and to run for safety on hearing the shout "incoming."

Sergeant Reckless receiving her promotion

BRETON

ADAPTABLE DRAFT HORSE

Horses have lived in the Breton mountains and moorlands of northwest France for thousands of years. The modern Breton horse has kept the hardiness of its ancestors but is much larger, due to crossbreeding with European and Asian breeds. Two distinct types of Breton horses are officially recognized: the Heavy Draft Breton, used to pull large and heavy loads, and the Postier Breton, known for its light and elegant gait.

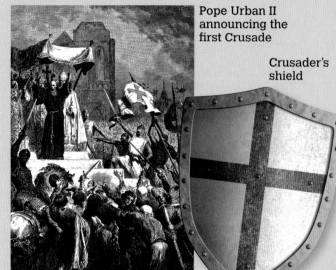

Pope Urban II announcing the first Crusade

Crusader's shield

Breed name: Breton

Other name: n/a

Breed purpose: farm work, especially in vineyards, draft

Size: 15.1–16 hands

Coat color: commonly red roan and chestnut, also bay and gray

Place of origin: Brittany, France

Ancestors: various, including Ardennais, Boulonnais, and Percheron

Up to the challenge

Postier Bretons, such as this one grazing on a farm in central France, are sturdy horses with exceptional energy levels, which were once the preferred breed of the French Horse Artillery. Unlike the more robust Heavy Draft Breton, used for the hardest work, Postier Bretons were used to pull mail coaches and for light farm work. Breton horses are still known for their ability under harness.

Crusading horses

In 1095, Pope Urban II launched the first Crusade—a war in which Christian armies from Europe battled to take over the area known as the Holy Land in the Middle East from its Islamic rulers. Knights from France fought on the backs of horses that were the ancestors of the modern Breton. The breed was strongly influenced by new blood lines of horses that were brought back from the Crusades.

In the **Crusades**, European **mountain horses** were **crossed** with horses from **the East** to create the **Bidet Breton**.

Festival horse

The Breton has been developed from native ancestral stock dating back thousands of years. It is still a regular sight at traditional festivals in Brittany, northwest France, as a symbol of the region's heritage. The horses are seen pulling decorated carriages and are themselves often covered in flowers.

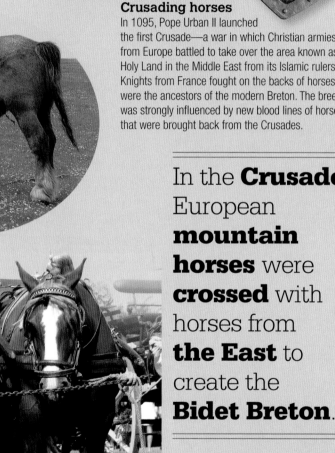

Desirable traits

Breton horses are popular breeding horses, and are often used to refine and improve other draft breeds. They have great stamina and strength, making them suitable for all kinds of agricultural work. They are also friendly, calm, and have an easy-going nature, characteristics that make them simple to train and great companions.

Branding

New foals are branded with a "cross and V" shape on the left side of the neck.

Elegant lines

Although it has the typical stout body of a draft horse, the Breton has an elegantly curved back.

Compact body

The Breton has a short barrel-shaped body and deep girth.

Coat colors

Red roan is the most common color of the Breton, often with a striking flaxen mane and tail. An attractive white blaze on the face is also a common feature.

Red roan

Bay

Chestnut

Gray

PERCHERON

RELIABLE DRAFT HORSE

The Percheron was the breed used by many different armies during World War I. An intelligent and obedient worker, thousands of the horses were killed on the battlefield during the conflict. Its numbers declined in the second half of the 20th century as farm machinery took over, but it remains a popular breed around the world. It is able to cope with a wide range of climates, and cross-bred Percherons are found in far-flung places, such as the Falkland Islands and northern Australia.

In **Disneyland, Paris**, teams of Percherons **pull trams** along **Main Street.**

Breed name: Percheron

Other name: n/a

Breed purpose: warhorse, draft, farm work, and riding

Breed size: 15.1–18.1 hands

Coat color: usually gray or black; sometimes chestnut, bay, and roan (US).

Place of origin: Le Perche, northwest France

Ancestors: unknown, possible Great Horse and Arab influence

Powerful body
The strong body is broad and deep-chested.

Hindquarters
The sloped, muscular quarters produce the power needed for heavy draft work.

Winning import
In 1873, the Duc de Chartres, a Percheron stallion, won first prize, the Grand Gold Medal, at the Concours Hippique Regional in Alençon, France. The horse was then acquired by American horse dealer August Rogy who took it back to Seward, Nebraska.

Light feathering
The well-muscled legs have little feathering on the lower parts.

Hooves and feet
The medium-sized feet are tipped with rounded hooves.

Under harness
Percheron teams are often used to pull carriages, for example sleighs at ski resorts. One of the most famous Percheron teams is the Heinz Hitch, which taies part in the Tournament of Roses Parade in Pasadena, California.

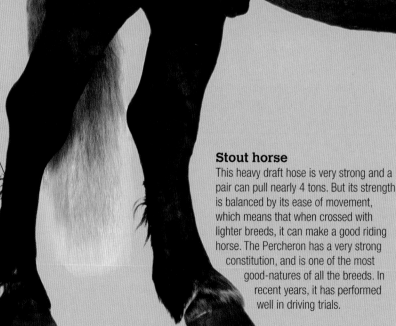

Stout horse
This heavy draft hose is very strong and a pair can pull nearly 4 tons. But its strength is balanced by its ease of movement, which means that when crossed with lighter breeds, it can make a good riding horse. The Percheron has a very strong constitution, and is one of the most good-natures of all the breeds. In recent years, it has performed well in driving trials.

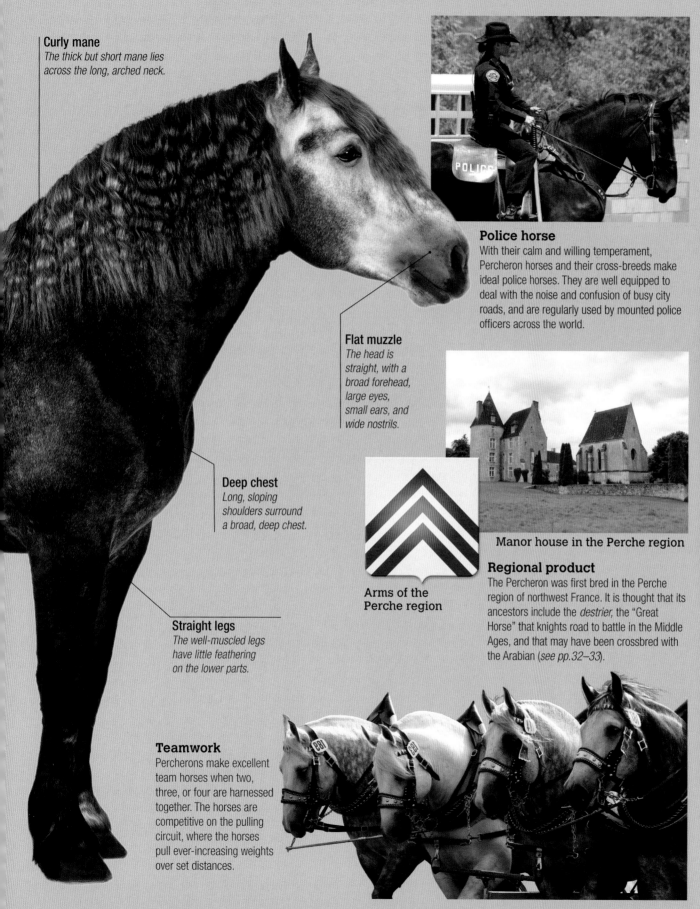

Curly mane
The thick but short mane lies across the long, arched neck.

Flat muzzle
The head is straight, with a broad forehead, large eyes, small ears, and wide nostrils.

Deep chest
Long, sloping shoulders surround a broad, deep chest.

Straight legs
The well-muscled legs have little feathering on the lower parts.

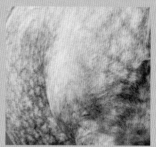

Police horse
With their calm and willing temperament, Percheron horses and their cross-breeds make ideal police horses. They are well equipped to deal with the noise and confusion of busy city roads, and are regularly used by mounted police officers across the world.

Coat colors
In France and the UK, only gray or black colors meet breed standards. In North America, chestnut, roan, and bay are allowed.

Dapple gray

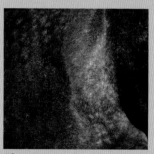

Black

Blue roan

Arms of the Perche region

Manor house in the Perche region

Regional product
The Percheron was first bred in the Perche region of northwest France. It is thought that its ancestors include the *destrier*, the "Great Horse" that knights road to battle in the Middle Ages, and that may have been crossbred with the Arabian (see pp.32–33).

Teamwork
Percherons make excellent team horses when two, three, or four are harnessed together. The horses are competitive on the pulling circuit, where the horses pull ever-increasing weights over set distances.

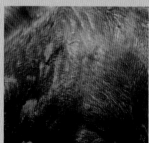

Chestnut

FRENCH HEAVY HORSES

A COUNTRY FAMED FOR AGRICULTURAL BREEDS

France has a long and proud tradition of producing hardy draft horses. As in other parts of the world, France's heavy breeds have seen a decline in numbers over recent decades, but they can still be seen under harness on farms and vineyards across the length and breadth of the country. Some breeds have enjoyed a revival in leisure and tourism, pulling carriages and giving rides, as the charms of these gentle creatures are rediscovered.

POITEVIN

POITOU, WEST-CENTRAL FRANCE

This breed is descended from horses brought to the Poitou region in the 17th century to help drain the marshes. It is often crossed with the Baudet de Poitou donkey to produce the strong, hard-working Poitevin mule. However, mule-breeding has contributed to the decline of the Poitevin and today, fewer than 100 new foals are born annually.

Breed name: Poitevin

Other name: Mulassier (mule-breeder)

Breed purpose: draft horse, producing mules

Size: 16–16.2 hands

Coat color: dun, gray, black, or bay

Place of origin: Poitou, France

Ancestors: Dutch, Norwegian, and Danish draft horses

Slow and steady

With large feet and slow, deliberate movements, the Poitevin horse was ideally suited to working in the soft, marshy conditions of Poitou. Today, those qualities make it a good horse to pull show carriages. In an effort to save the breed, herds have been reintroduced to French marshlands.

AUXOIS

BURGUNDY, EAST-CENTRAL FRANCE

The Auxois is rarely seen outside its native Burgundy. It has a calm temperament and is noted for its endurance. Despite these qualities, it has never been exported outside France, and is now the rarest of the nine French draft breeds. To raise its profile, an annual breed show is held in France.

Breed name: Auxois

Other name: n/a

Breed purpose: draft horse, meat

Size: 15.3–16.3 hands

Coat color: mostly bay or bay roan

Place of origin: Burgundy, France

Ancestors: Bourguignon, Ardennais, Percheron, Boulonnais

Close to home
The Auxois is closely related to the similar Ardennais breed. Auxois numbers dipped dramatically in the mid 20th century, and by 1970, it was nearly extinct. The French government are trying to turn this around, using Auxois horses for leisure and tourism.

COMTOIS

FRANCH-COMTÉ, EASTERN FRANCE

Originating in the Jura Mountains on the border between France and Switzerland, the Comtois is known as a fast learner and willing worker, and has become the most popular of the French heavy breeds. It is still used in farming, hauling logs in the Jura pine forests and working the hilly vineyards of eastern France.

Breed name: Comtois

Other name: n/a

Breed purpose: farm work

Breed size: 14.2–16 hands

Coat color: chestnut

Place of origin: Franche-Comté, France

Ancestors: interbred with Norman, Boulonnais, and Ardennais

Lightening up
In recent years, the Comtois has become a popular leisure horse, and the breeding focus has been to produce a lighter horse more suited to riding. Sought-after traits include the breed's strong legs, muscular hindquarters, and long, straight back.

BOULONNAIS

PAS DE CALAIS, NORTHERN FRANCE

Once a common working horse, the Boulonnais fell out of favor after World War II. It has enjoyed a revival since the 1970s, and a recent cross-breed known as the Araboulonnais has proved particularly popular. A cross between the Boulonnais and Arabians, it combines the gentle temperament of a draft horse with the spirit of an Arab.

Breed name: Boulonnais

Other name: White Marble Horse

Breed purpose: transport and agriculture

Size: 15.1–17.3 hands

Coat color: mostly gray, occasionally chestnut

Place of origin: Pas de Calais, northern France

Ancestors: unknown

Fish carrier
Between the 17th and early 20th century, a quick-trotting Boulonnais type known as the *mareyeur* (fish merchant) was used to provide the fast transport of fish from the port of Boulogne to the Paris markets.

ARDENNAIS

ANCIENT WARHORSE

This powerful breed has been shaped by the harsh winters of the Ardennes, a region that has produced tough horses for thousands of years. The robust nature of the Ardennais' ancestors was highly regarded by Julius Caesar, who began using them in warfare in the 1st century BCE.

Breed name: Ardennais

Other names: Ardennes Horse

Breed purpose: warhorse, forestry

Breed size: 15.3 hands

Coat color: various colors, excluding black

Place of origin: Ardennes region, France and Belgium

Ancestors: possibly the ancient Solutre horse, some Arabian blood

When **he invaded** the Ardennes in **57 BCE**, Julius Caesar described the region's horses as "**rustic, hard, and tireless**."

Calm companion
The Ardennais horse is known for being easy to handle and is gentle enough for children and people who are nervous around horses. Its compact and muscular body developed to suit the harsh life in the wilds of the Ardennes Mountains, where winters can be severe. Its steady gait and willing nature can be reassuring for young or inexperienced riders.

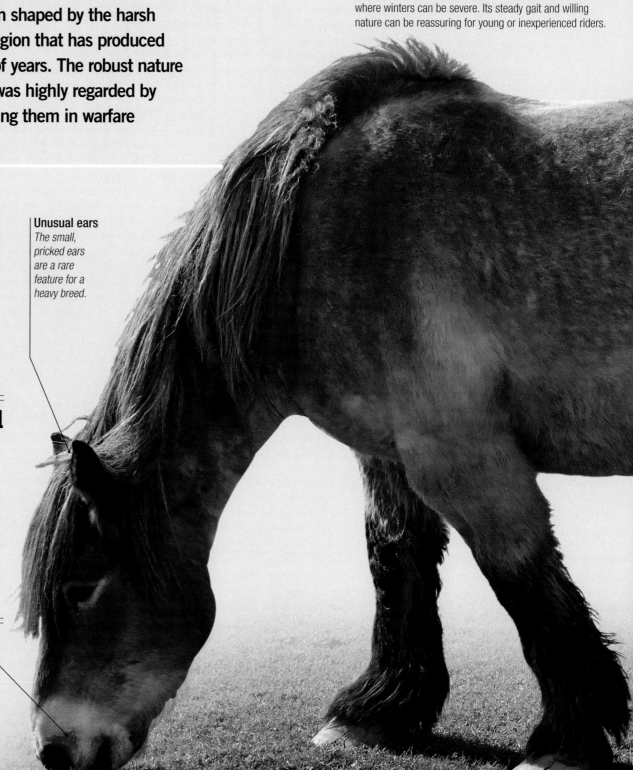

Unusual ears
The small, pricked ears are a rare feature for a heavy breed.

Noble nose
The face of an Ardennais is recognizable by its squared-off nose.

Tractorlike body
The back is unusually short, even for a draft horse, and it is flanked by very muscular loins. It has been described as being "built like a tractor."

Big bones
The Ardennais is noted for its massive skeletal structure, which makes it extremely robust.

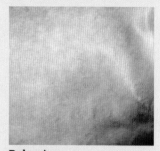

Artillery horse
It was not only the Romans that valued these horses on the battlefield. The Ardennais gained a reputation for toughness during the Napoleonic Wars in Europe during the early 19th century. French emperor Napoleon added Arab blood to the breed to improve its endurance. His horses were among the few to survive the French army's disastrous winter retreat from Moscow in 1812 (above).

Coat colors
The breed standard for the Ardennais prefers roan, red roan, iron gray, bay, and dark or liver chestnut. Bay-brown and palomino are also allowed, but black and dapple gray are not allowed in this breed.

Palomino

Liver chestnut

Bay

International breed
The Ardennais has been exported to many countries to carry out a range of tasks. Some of the most common uses include farm and forestry work. In Sweden, Ardennais horses are widely used to pull logs as part of forest management. Because of its stamina and mild temper, the breed is increasingly used in competitive driving across Europe.

Popular import

A Belgian Draft Horse gallops through a field in New England, US. The US version of this breed was first developed by a group of three businessmen from Wabash, Indiana, who formed a company to import the horses from Belgium in 1937. Today, there are more Belgian Draft Horses in the United States than all other breeds of heavy horse put together.

BELGIAN HEAVY DRAFT

A HIT IN EUROPE AND THE US

Through strictly controlled breeding, the Belgian Heavy Draft has been developed into a powerful but versatile draft horse that is popular in both Europe and North America. They are still employed as working horses, but are also talented show horses, and are regularly seen in pulling contests.

Heavyweight worker
These horses are incredibly strong and can pull a wagon that weighs up to 8,000 pounds (3,600 kg), which is around 4 tons. They are also exceptionally tough and hard-working, and are able to keep going for long hours—working up to 10 hours a day.

Breed name: Belgian Heavy Draft

Other names: Brabant, Brabander, Belgian Horse

Breed purpose: farm work, draft, and harness work

Size: average 16.2–17 hands

Coat color: chestnut, palomino, bay, and roan

Place of origin: Belgium

Ancestors: Flemish, possibly Great Horse

Pair of horses under harness

Refined looks
The head is lightweight in comparison to the thick-set body.

Strong and sensitive
This breed is surprisingly docile and easy-to-handle, with young horses that are playful in nature. Its build makes it well suited to all sorts of draft work, from plowing to pulling wagons. It is muscular, with a light, square head, broad back, and feathering on the lower legs.

Belgian Heavy Drafts are said to be **descended** from the *destriers*, **warhorses** that carried **medieval knights** into battle.

Collecting shrimp
Every summer in Oostduinkerke, a seaside resort in western Belgium, these draft horses can be seen wading through the shallow water with fishermen on their backs, dragging fishing nets behind them. The nets are trawling for gray shrimp, which are used to make a local delicacy known as *tomate-crevettes*.

Fluffy fetlocks
European Belgians typically have thick feathering.

Working weight
The horse has a powerful, well-formed body with strong shoulders and neck.

Belgian Heavy Draft cantering across sand

Time capsule

These two powerful Belgian Heavy Draft horses are pulling a farm wagon. They are at the Howell Living History Farm in Lambertville, New Jersey, which recreates farm life as it was lived here in the period 1890–1910. Gasoline-powered technology was beginning to take over, so this way of life was threatened. On a farm like this one, horses were used to provide power to plow, plant, cultivate, and reap. They were also used for all transportation, either as draft horses pulling carts or carriages, or as riding horses for the farmers.

JUTLAND

JUTLAND, DENMARK

An attractive, thick-set draft horse, the Jutland breed was developed in Denmark in the 19th century as a farm worker. From a peak of around 50,000 in 1950, only about 1,000 horses remain today. A team of Jutlands can still be seen at work pulling wagons on the streets of the Danish capital city, Copenhagen.

Breed name: Jutland

Other name: Judsk, Danish

Breed purpose: farmwork

Breed size: 15–16.1 hands

Coat color: chestnut

Country/place of origin: Jutland, Denmark

Ancestors: Viking horses, Suffolk Punch

Viking ancestors

The Jutland is thought to be descended from Viking warhorses. The modern breed was developed by introducing new blood, most notably the Suffolk Punch from Britain, itself also thought to be descended from Viking stock.

Firm base
The short, thick legs have heavy feathering around the cannon bone and withers.

Lookalike
With its flaxen mane and chestnut coloring, the Jutland is very similar in appearance to the Suffolk Punch.

Jutland horse in its thick winter coat

Jutland foal with a white blaze

DØLE GUDBRANDSDAL

NORWAY

A small, compact draft breed, the Døle Gudbrandstal was originally developed as a pack horse to carry goods along an overland trade route between Norway's capital city Oslo and the North Sea. For a horse of its size, it has a remarkable pulling ability. A lighter type known as the Døle Trotter is bred for harness racing.

Breed name: Døle Gudbrandsdal

Other name: Dølehest

Breed purpose: pack horse

Breed size: 15 hands

Coat color: black, brown, and bay

Country/place of origin: Norway

Ancestors: several, including Friesian

Preserving the breed
Following a steep decline in its numbers, a breeding center was established in 1962 to preserve the Døle Gudbrandstal, and about 200 new foals are registered each year.

NORTH SWEDISH

SWEDEN

The central stud for the North Swedish Horse was established in Wången, Sweden, in 1903 to create a robust breed for forestry work. Wången is also the center for Swedish harness racing, and a lighter type of the North Swedish Horse, known as the Scandinavian Coldblood Trotter, has found huge success in trotting races.

Breed name: North Swedish Horse

Other name: n/a

Breed purpose: forestry

Breed size: 16 hands

Coat color: mostly brown or black, but any solid color

Country/place of origin: Northern Sweden

Ancestors: Døle Gudbrandsdal and others

Heavy testing
The Wången stud operates a strict breeding program in which horses are tested by hauling loads over rough ground. This has produced an exceptionally strong draft horse.

DUTCH DRAFT

NETHERLANDS

Developed by cross-breeding Belgian horses with local Zeeland stock in the early 20th century, the Dutch Draft is a massive horse. Although its numbers have dropped, it can still be seen on farms around the Netherlands.

Breed name: Dutch Draft

Other name: Dutch Heavy Draft Horse, Zeeland Horse

Breed purpose: farmwork and forestry

Breed size: 16 hands

Coat color: chestnut, bay, and gray

Country/place of origin: Netherlands

Ancestors: Zeeland, Belgian Draft, Ardennais

Slow and steady
The Dutch Draft is renowned for its exceptionally calm temperament, and while it is slow in pace, it has the stamina to keep going all day.

A way of life

Amish farmers in North America still farm without the use of modern machinery. Preferring traditional methods, they keep draft horses, typically powerful breeds such as the Percheron or the Belgian draft horse. For lighter draft work, such as haymaking (pictured above), they may use mules. Outside the farm, the Amish travel on public highways in horse-drawn carriages as they prefer not to drive motorized vehicles.

ON THE FARM

Horses and other equines have long been used on farms, pulling plows or carrying goods to market. Heavy draft breeds were developed to cope with the workload. In some parts of the world, horses were also bred for their meat. On many farms today, the jobs once performed by horses are now done with machinery, and the numbers of most draft breeds have declined sharply.

Milk and meat

The first people to domesticate horses, the Botai, lived on the Steppes grasslands of modern-day Kazakhstan more than 5,000 years ago. Archaeologists have discovered pottery made by the Botai that has traces of horse milk and horse fat. This shows that they milked the mares and that they also ate horsemeat. Bones found at Botai settlements prove that the animals were pony-sized, around 13–14 hands at the withers, and that they were the ancestors of the wild Przewalski's horse.

Steppes grasslands, Kazakhstan

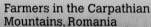
Skull of a Przewalski's horse

A rich fertilizer

Horse dung makes an excellent organic fertilizer, and many farmers sell their manure to local gardeners. A single horse produces about 50 pounds (20 kg) of dung in a day. That is 8 tons a year! The manure needs about two or three months to rot down into compost before it is added to the soil. This destroys potentially harmful germs, leaving chemicals such as nitrates that plants need to grow.

Well-rotted compost full of nutrients for plants

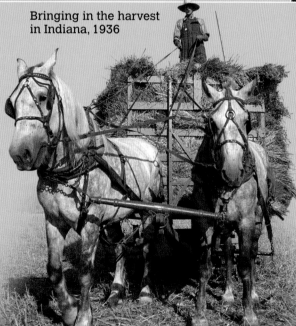
Bringing in the harvest in Indiana, 1936

Recent revival

Draft horses continue to be employed on farms in remote mountainous areas, where heavy machinery is difficult to use on the uneven ground. By contrast, sure-footed mountain horses can easily climb hills and maneuver around rocky terrain. Horses have also enjoyed a revival at lower altitudes in recent years. Some small farmers find that horses are cheaper and easier to keep than a tractor.

Farmers in the Carpathian Mountains, Romania

Rise and fall of the draft

Draft horses such as Percherons, Shires, and Belgians were shipped from Europe to the US in the 1800s to work on the country's rapidly expanding farms. Horses helped with plowing and transportation, as well as powering threshing machines. By 1920, there were around 25 million horses on US farms, but this number had dropped to 4 million by 1954. That same year, the number of tractors on US farms hit 5 million.

Cultivating corn in California, 1937

NORIKER

MOUNTAIN BREED

For more than 1,000 years, the ancestors of the Noriker played an important role in European trade, carrying goods from Austria across the Alps to the Adriatic Sea. The modern breed has inherited the power and endurance of its ancient ancestors, but has a more refined look as a result of the introduction of Spanish blood from the 16th century.

Breed name: Noriker

Other names: Norico-Pinzgauer, Pinzgauer

Breed purpose: pack horse, forestry

Breed size: 15.1–16.3 hands

Coat color: chestnut, bay, black, brown, and spotted

Place of origin: Austria

Ancestors: ancient breed, probably brought from Greece, with some Spanish and Neapolitan influence

Enduring popularity
While draft horses have all but disappeared from most parts of Europe, around 10,000 Noriker horses remain in Austria. Its mountainous terrain is less well suited to heavy machinery than other regions, and foresters in the Alps still employ large numbers of these horses.

Bareback contest
During religious festivals in the southern Austrian state of Carinthia, young men take part in a mounted contest called the Kufensteken. Riding bareback on a Noriker horse, each contestant rides past a barrel wrapped in hazel rings and strikes it with a metal bat in an attempt to cut the rings.

Strong quarters
Powerful muscles make this a capable pack horse.

Clean limbs
The relatively short legs have little or no feathering.

The Noriker is named after **Noricum**, a **Celtic kingdom** that was conquered by **the Romans** in the **1st century** CE.

High pastures
The ancestral Norikers were brought to Austria from Greece by the ancient Romans. Over the course of the last 2,000 years, they have slowly changed into a very hardy, heavy breed suited to extreme conditions. The horses are still raised on high mountain pastures at 6,000 ft (1,830 meters). They are kept outdoors all year round and rarely need extra feed.

Noriker on a mountain pasture in the Alps

Muscular neck
The strong neck makes the breed an ideal one for work under harness.

Solid head
The square, thick-set head becomes thinner toward the muzzle.

Deep chest
A broad, deep girth gives the horse a low center of gravity, which helps to make it very sure-footed in the mountains.

Coat colors
The wide variety of coat colors contributes to the Noriker's popularity. In addition to the basic colors bay, black, brown, and chestnut, some are spotted or roan. There are no gray Norikers.

Leopard

Brown

Chestnut

Leopard coat
Some Norikers have a coat pattern known as *leopard complex.* The pattern consists of colored spots on a white coat. The whole coat may show this pattern, or the horse may have a spotted "blanket" over just part of the body. Leopard Norikers are highly prized.

BLACK FOREST HORSE

GERMANY
GERMANY

This striking breed was developed about 200 years ago to work in the Black Forest in southern Germany. The main center for the breed is the Marbach Stud in Baden-Württemberg, Germany's oldest state stud farm. Since 2001, Black Forest Horses have also been bred in the US.

Breed name: Black Forest Horse	**Place of origin:** Baden-Württemberg, Germany
Other name: Black Forest Coldblood	**Ancestors:** local Black Forest horses such as the Wälderpferd
Breed purpose: forestry	
Size: 14.1–15.3 hands	
Coat color: dark chestnut	

Under harness
The Black Forest Horse is a popular choice for work under harness. During winter in the Black Forest, it can be seen pulling sleighs. Its thick, flaxen mane makes it an easy breed to spot.

ITALIAN HEAVY DRAFT

ITALY

Hardy and fast-moving, the Italian Heavy Draft is ideally suited to general farmwork, but its numbers declined sharply with the mechanization of agriculture. It can still be seen working on farms in mountainous parts of Italy.

Breed name: Italian Heavy Draft	**Coat color:** chestnut, roan, bay
Other name: Quick Heavy Draft	**Place of origin:** Italy
Breed purpose: farmwork	**Ancestors:** include Brabant and Breton
Size: 15–16 hands	

Fast breed
As its alternative name suggests, the Italian Heavy Draft is particularly noted for its speed, which made it suitable for a range of draft work on farms and in the military. The mares are often used to breed mules, which inherit the horses' swift movement.

Made for the mountains

The Freiberger has the typical features of a horse bred in the mountains, with sure feet and great balance. This good-looking breed is showcased every August at a festival in the Swiss canton (state) of Saignelégier in the Freiberg Mountains.

FREIBERGER

SWITZERLAND

Classed as either a light coldblood or a heavy warmblood, the Freiberger was developed as a versatile workhorse for the Swiss Army, which still uses it in small numbers. It is bred at the Swiss National Stud Farm in Avenches, which is now a center for equine research.

Breed name: Freiberger	**Coat color:** bay, dark bay, or chestnut
Other name: Franches-Montagnes	**Place of origin:** Switzerland
Breed purpose: farmwork, pack horse	**Ancestors:** Anglo-Norman stock, the extinct Norfolk Roadster
Size: 15 hands	

SOUTH GERMAN COLDBLOOD

GERMANY

A close relative of the Austrian Noriker (*see pp.176–177*), the South German has quicker, more agile movement than most draft breeds as a result of the introduction of warmblood lines. It also has strong legs and hard hooves.

Breed name: South German Coldblood

Other name: Süddeutsches Kaltblut

Breed purpose: farm work, forestry

Size: 16–16.2 hands

Coat color: chestnut

Place of origin: southern Germany

Ancestors: Noriker, probable Thoroughbred

Bavarian beauty

With around 2,000 breeding mares, the South German Coldblood is the most numerous of Germany's four draft breeds. It is found mostly in Bavaria, where grazing horses are still a common sight.

SCHLESWIG

SCHLESWIG-HOLSTEIN, GERMANY

This heavy breed from northern Germany was bred from Jutland horses (*see p.172*) in the 19th century as a draft horse for forestry and agriculture. Its traditional jobs have since disappeared, and Schleswig numbers have dropped to critically low levels.

Fast learner

A medium-sized breed, the Scheswig has a short head and broad forehead, with the short, powerful neck that is typical of draft horses. It has a reputation for intelligence and versatility, and is considered to be a fast and willing learner.

Breed name: Schleswig	**Coat color:** chestnut, gray, bay
Other name: Schleswig Coldblood	**Place of origin:** Schleswig-Holstein, Germany
Breed purpose: farmwork and forestry	**Ancestors:** Jutland, Suffolk Punch
Breed size: 15.2–16 hands	

SOKOLSKI

POLAND

The Sokolski was developed in Poland at the start of the 20th century. Various draft breeds were crossed to produce a powerful animal capable of heavy draft and farm work. Full of energy and willing to work, it is known to be an very easy horse to keep. It has now largely been replaced by tractors, but its muscular pulling power can still be admired at horse shows.

Breed name: Sokolski

Other name: Sokolsky

Breed purpose: heavy draft work

Size: 15–16 hands

Coat color: bay, brown, chestnut

Place of origin: northeast Poland

Ancestors: local horses crossed with other draft breeds, including Ardennais, Anglo-Norman, Døle Gudbrandstal, and Belgian Heavy Draft

Muscular and strong
The Sokolski is a modern breed that was created following a long tradition of draft horses in its native Poland. It met a growing need for horses that could both pull heavy loads and move quickly over longer distances.

Fast grower
The Russian Heavy Draft grows very quickly, reaching nearly its full height by the time it is 18 months old. It has a long life expectancy and can carry on working right into old age.

RUSSIAN HEAVY DRAFT

UKRAINE

Short and muscular, this draft horse was bred to survive the harsh winters of the Russian Empire. The breed was significantly improved in the 1950s by the state studs in Ukraine, then part of the Soviet Union. Breeders crossed Ukrainian mares with Ardennais, Brabant, and Percheron stallions. The result was the strongest draft horse for its weight of any Soviet breed.

Breed name: Russian Heavy Draft

Other name: Russian Ardennes

Breed purpose: farm work

Size: 14.1–15 hands

Coat color: roan, bay, and chestnut

Place of origin: Ukraine

Ancestors: native Ukrainian breeds, Ardennais, Brabant, Percheron, Orlov Trotter

Milk drink
The Russian Heavy Draft is still kept today for its milk, which is used to make Kumis, a drink made from fermented mare's milk that is said to have medicinal qualities.

VLADIMIR

NORTHEAST RUSSIA

Developed in the first half of the 20th century from three Clydesdale foundation stallions, the Vladimir is a strong draft horse with a deep girth, ideally suited to heavy farm work. Despite its solid build, it is noted for a lively action, and combines pulling power with speed.

Breed name: Vladimir Heavy Draft

Other name: Russian Clydesdale

Breed purpose: farmwork

Size: 16.1 hands

Coat color: bay, chestnut

Place of origin: northeast Russia

Ancestor: Clydesdale

Rounded belly
More solidly built than its Clydesdale ancestors, the Vladimir has a particularly deep girth.

Healthy breed
A well-formed horse with a thick black mane, the Vladimir usually has a white blaze or star on its face. It is known to be a sturdy breed that matures quickly and has few health problems.

Troika racing
With its high action, the Vladimir has proved a popular breed in the Russian sport of troika racing, in which a carriage is pulled by three horses. The middle horse runs at a fast trot, while the two outer horses canter.

CARE OF

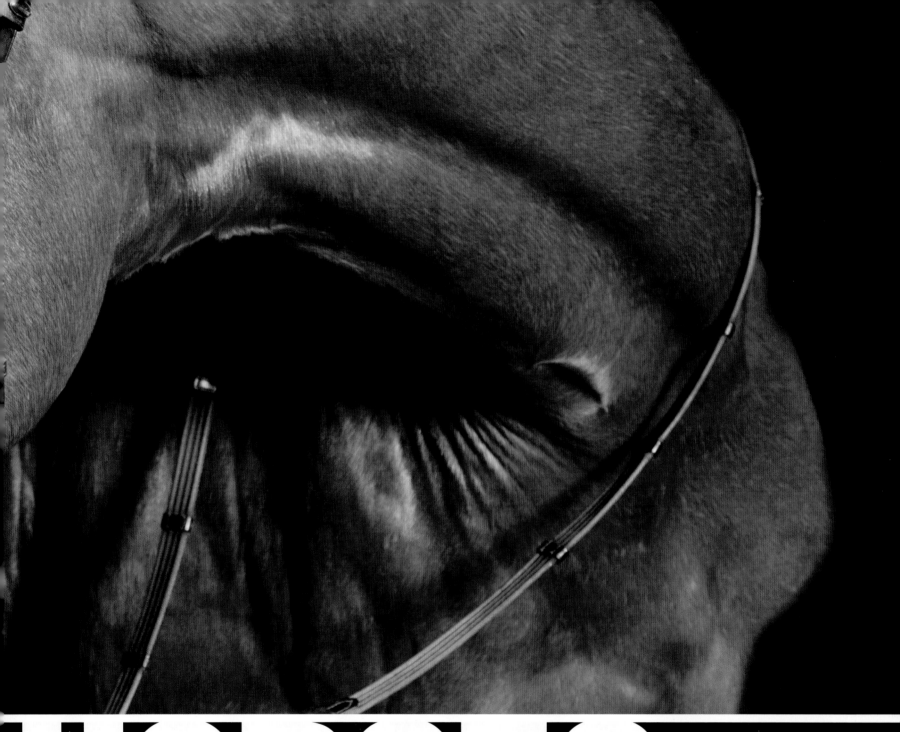

HORSES

Understanding a horse

It is important to understand a horse's behavior when you are keeping them in a stable. A horse with pricked ears and clear eyes looking around the yard over the stable door tells you that the animal is alert, interested, and happy. If stall kicking, pawing, weaving, and attempting to bite over the door is going on, these may be caused by boredom from being kept in the stall.

LOOKING AFTER HORSES

KEEPING HORSES FIT, HEALTHY, AND HAPPY

Many more hours are spent looking after a horse than are spent riding it, but devoted horse owners do not mind this. Feeding, grooming, turning out are all activities that build trust between horse and owner, and form a strong relationship that will last for many years.

Owning a horse is a dream come true for many owners, but it requires real commitment. It means early starts day in day out in all weathers, even in the depths of winter, to check the horse, feed it, and turn out its stable. Even if a horse or pony is out in a field it will need checking twice a day. Horses have to have the right feed and bedding. They need regular grooming, and it is important to be alert to any changes that might indicate that they are ill and need a visit from a vet.

Some people are lucky enough to have their own land and stables. However, many people pay to keep their horse in livery. Livery yards may either simply provide a stable and paddock, or they may take over full care of a horse, apart from when the owner chooses to do it or wants a ride. If an owner has the time to fully care for their horse, this pays dividends in that it develops a strong relationship between them.

Getting equipped
Learning to ride means acquiring all the right equipment. A correctly fitting riding hat is one essential the rider cannot be without. Riding boots and body protectors may also be useful.

Horses benefit from a regular routine, so it is as well to establish that from day one. They need shelter, whether in a stable yard or out in a field. It is vital that they have lots of exercise, so being allowed to run free in a paddock as well as being ridden regularly ensures their well-being. Horses must also have plenty of water and a balanced diet. In the wild, they wander about and graze on grass and other plants, often and in small quantities. Their digestive systems need this roughage, and stabled horses should be provided with grass or hay, as well as feeds that contain blended cereals and other ingredients to give them the energy that they need. It is important to match the amount of feed to the level of work that is being asked of the horse.

A domesticated horse has an average life expectancy of 25 to 30 years—plenty of time to build a really great relationship between this most magnificent of animals and its owner.

"Riding a horse is not a gentle hobby. . . . It is a grand passion."
Ralph Waldo Emerson

Royal Moroccan stables, 18th century

Mare and foal in the stable

Line-up on the tackroom wall

Examination by a vet

EXERCISE, PASTURE, AND SHELTER

BASIC NEEDS FOR A HEALTHY HORSE

A healthy horse is a happy horse, and there are many different ways to make sure that your horse stays on top form throughout its life. How a horse is kept and how often it is turned out to pasture depends on what the horse is used for—competition horses, for example, will need almost constant attention. This is because they traditionally spend more time inside a stable, where they are less likely to injure themselves, and can get bored and frustrated. The essentials for any horse's physical and mental state of health are plenty of exercise, grass to graze on, and a comfortable place to rest.

Daily rides

A horse cannot be left all day in its stable because it will get bored, its muscles will stiffen, and it may have problems digesting food. A daily ride or walk will keep it fit and healthy. It is important to regularly saddle up a horse that is ridden. This helps to keep its back and girth in good condition.

Bracken

Buttercups

Tansy ragwort

Weed watch

A grassy paddock is likely to be dotted with clover and weeds. Usually, this is fine and adds a variety of exciting tastes and textures to a horse's diet. However, some plants are poisonous to horses, including bracken and the wild flowers tansy ragwort and buttercup. A horse will usually stay clear of these toxic plants, but they should be removed if spotted.

Happy horses in their stable

A multi-sectioned stable

No place like home

A horse's stable is like a person's bedroom—it should feel clean, comfortable, and safe. Many stables are designed as enclosed boxes and stalls inside a larger barn complex. Stable boxes can either face outward onto a yard, or inward, so that the horses can see one another. Stables should always be well-ventilated, properly drained, and protected from the weather.

Hold your horses

Horses are talented escape artists. It is important to make sure that paddocks and stables are safe and secure. Post and rail fencing make effective paddock boundaries. Banks and hedges provide additional shelter from wind and rain.

Dirty work

Bedding in a stable is vital for a variety of reasons. It prevents injury to feet and legs, stops drafts, provides warmth and comfort, and encourages the horse to urinate. However, it is essential that the stable is mucked out regularly and clean, absorbent bedding put in place. If this does not happen, the horse may develop respiratory problems from damp or wet bedding.

Clean routine

Horses are naturally clean animals, and they will not eat near their droppings. Their stables should be mucked out regularly to keep them clean, dry, and mold free. Hemp, wood shavings, straw, and shredded paper are good bedding choices. They are absorbent and dust free, and a horse will not eat them.

Wood shavings

Straw

Shredded paper

Hemp

Glorious grazing

Grass is a horse's favorite food and it will happily spend all day munching away at the stuff. Grazing also helps a horse stay happy and healthy by providing it with gentle exercise and the opportunity to socialize with other horses. Grass is also the most economical food for horses as it is hardy and grows fast.

DIET AND FEEDING

FINDING THE RIGHT BALANCE

A good diet is crucial to a horse's wellbeing and ability to perform or work. Horses are natural herbivores, which means that they only eat plants such as grass and gorse. All this roughage is very difficult to digest, and a lot of what a horse eats would be indigestible to humans. However, horses have specially adapted digestive systems that allow them to gain enough energy from their diet to fuel them throughout the day.

Food and water

Every horse should have drinking water available at all times. The water needs to be fresh as the horse may refuse to drink if it notices a change in the taste. Horses have sensitive stomachs and do not like changing their diet. If they have too much concentrated food or dry mix, they can become over excitable. If they do not have access to grass or hay to graze on, they can feel stressed.

Hungry as a horse
Horses prefer to eat small amounts of food steadily throughout the day. A horse's stomach empties every 15 minutes, so it needs to keep topping it up. Dry mixes have the protein, fiber, starch, and nutrients to keep the horse satisfied for longer.

Eating on the move

Enjoying hay from a trough

In its **natural habitat**, a horse **moves slowly** to **save energy**, and will **graze** on **grass and shrubs** for **12-20 hours** a day.

Dietary extras
All horses and ponies need salt, which comes in the form of a mineral block. The horses gnaw or lick the block either in their stalls or out in the paddock. Some essential fat can be provided by oils, which can be added to the horses' feed.

Types of food
Alongside their dry mix and coat conditioning foods such as linseeds, horses love healthy treats. Apples, carrots, and pumpkins, cut up small, are some of their favorites.

Chaff

Linseeds

Pellets

Dry mix

Adapting diets
Every horse is different, and needs the right food and water for its size, age, and activity level. A growing foal will need lots of nutrients, as will a horse that is pregnant or producing milk. Riding horses often use more energy than horses in the wild, so they will need to be fed extra calories and nutrients to match.

Perkiness
A horse with pricked ears is a horse that is alert and interested in its surroundings.

Bright eyes
Your horse's eyes should be clear and bright, not cloudy or discolored.

Healthy coat
A shiny coat is a sign of good health, showing that the horse is well fed and groomed regularly.

Clean nostrils
An excessive discharge from the nostrils may indicate a problem.

HEALTH AND HEALTHCARE
YOUR HORSE'S WELLBEING

Despite their size and strength, horses can be delicate creatures and are prone to various health problems. A healthy horse will have a shiny coat, bright eyes, pricked ears, and appear in good spirits. It should be agile in movement, and happy to walk and run around its paddock. Changes in behavior and any signs of discomfort should be investigated straight away.

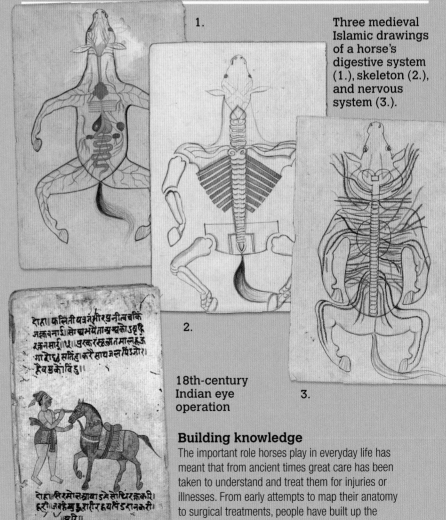

1.

Three medieval Islamic drawings of a horse's digestive system (1.), skeleton (2.), and nervous system (3.).

2.

3.

18th-century Indian eye operation

Picture of health
You need to keep your horse fit and well, and preventing problems should be top of your agenda. Make sure your horse is up to date with vaccinations against infectious diseases, that the stable and stableyard are clean, and that the pasture or paddock is free of poisonous plants.

Building knowledge
The important role horses play in everyday life has meant that from ancient times great care has been taken to understand and treat them for injuries or illnesses. From early attempts to map their anatomy to surgical treatments, people have built up the knowledge and skills that make today's vets invaluable.

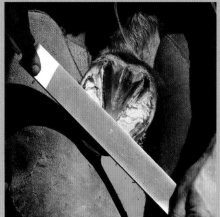
Hooves being filed to a flat surface to take the shoe

Every horse owner **should know** their horse's normal, healthy **resting temperature**, heart rate, **breathing pattern**, the **color** of **their gums**, and **other vital signs**.

Hammering holes for the fixing nails into the red-hot shoe

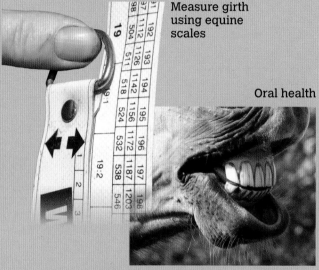

Measure girth using equine scales

Oral health

Pressing the hot shoe into the hoof—this does not harm the horse

Regular checkups

There are several vital checks needed to keep a horse healthy. Body weight can be judged by taking measurements and the horse's diet changed if necessary. Teeth need to be checked for uneven growth that might need attention from an equine dentist. And pink gums are healthy, while pale, blue, or yellow gums are a warning of ill-health.

Made to measure

A horse hoof is made of keratin, which is the same substance that human nails are made of. Heavily worked horses have traditionally been given metal shoes to protect the keratin from wearing down. Metal shoes are becoming less popular as they are not thought to be good for the horse. Rubber shoes are increasingly common, and some horses may even go shoeless.

The shoe being nailed into the hoof

The finished shoe on the hoof

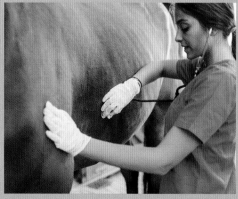

Call the vet

Get to know the behavior of your horse and have it checked out by the vet if you notice anything out of the ordinary. Changes in behavior, physical appearance, or eating and drinking habits can be signs of problems.

Horse care on the battlefield

Throughout history, farriers have had to carry out their work in some very strange places, but none of them more dangerous than a battlefield. This farrier is working at the military headquarters set up by the Union army of the North during the Battle of Antietam in September 1862. Not only did he have to shoe thousands of horses of many different breeds and temperaments, but he also had to use any knowledge he had to provide the horses with medical care for any illnesses and injuries. During the American Civil War (1861–1865), an estimated 1.5 million horses and mules perished.

GROOMING
ESSENTIAL DAILY CARE

Most horses love to be groomed—if done correctly. Grooming should be done regularly—a horse should always be cleaned before being ridden as a dirty coat will rub under a saddle and create sores. With teeth, hooves, and coats preened to perfection, a horse will perform at its best.

Bonding ritual
In the wild, horses like to groom one another by gently biting each other's coat. This keeps them healthy and helps them to bond with each other. Owners can bond with their horses during grooming, building a level of trust that makes the horse easier to ride.

A wash and brush-up
There are many different types of brushes used for grooming. First, a curry comb loosens any mud and dirt and a dandy brush sweeps it away. Then, a body brush removes dust, dry skin, and loose hair. A soft body brush is swept around the face and ears, and a comb is used on the mane and tail. Mud is removed from the soles of the hooves with a hoof pick.

Having a shower to cool off

An equine groom's equipment box

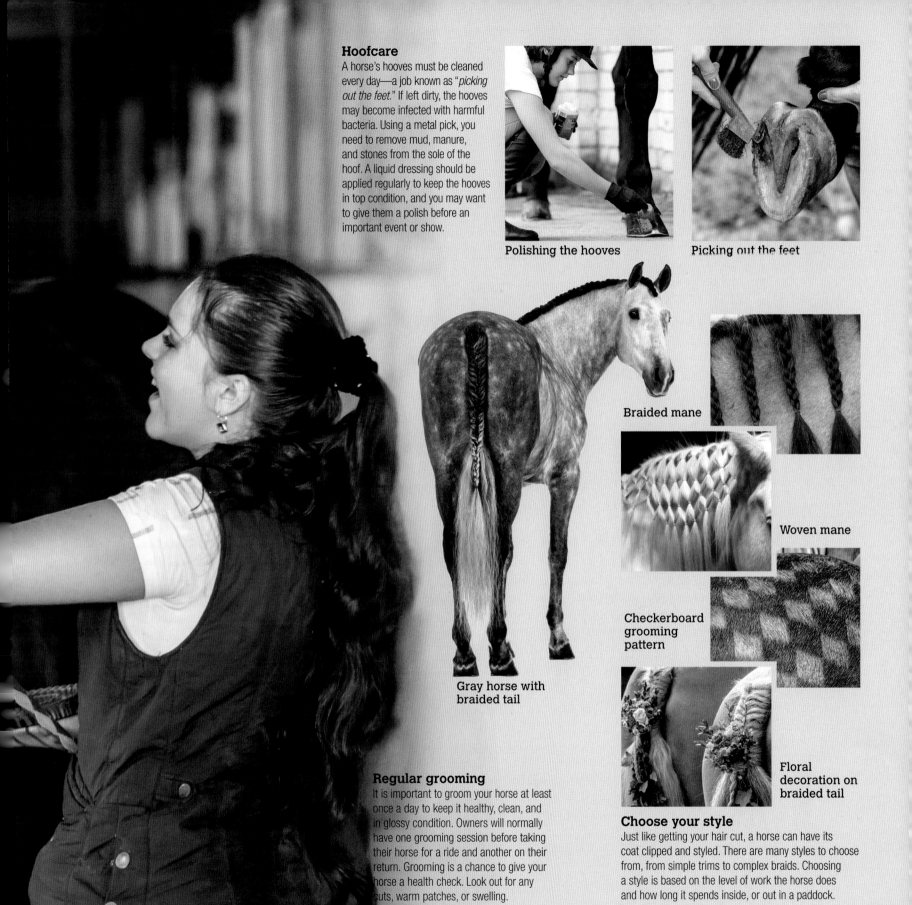

Hoofcare

A horse's hooves must be cleaned every day—a job known as "*picking out the feet.*" If left dirty, the hooves may become infected with harmful bacteria. Using a metal pick, you need to remove mud, manure, and stones from the sole of the hoof. A liquid dressing should be applied regularly to keep the hooves in top condition, and you may want to give them a polish before an important event or show.

Polishing the hooves

Picking out the feet

Braided mane

Woven mane

Checkerboard grooming pattern

Gray horse with braided tail

Floral decoration on braided tail

Regular grooming

It is important to groom your horse at least once a day to keep it healthy, clean, and in glossy condition. Owners will normally have one grooming session before taking their horse for a ride and another on their return. Grooming is a chance to give your horse a health check. Look out for any cuts, warm patches, or swelling.

Choose your style

Just like getting your hair cut, a horse can have its coat clipped and styled. There are many styles to choose from, from simple trims to complex braids. Choosing a style is based on the level of work the horse does and how long it spends inside, or out in a paddock.

Double delight

Whether you are an owner, a weekend rider, get excited watching
horse races and competitions, or simply enjoy reading about horses
and ponies, you cannot fail to fall in love with these animals. For
thousands of years, they have been faithful companions, willing to
carry people and goods, pull carts and carriages, and work hard on
farms and in forests. Today, with modern machinery taking away most
of the grueling work, horses and ponies are used mostly for pleasure,
and our bond with them is more personal, caring, and long-lasting.

amble
A gait used by some horses in which both left legs and both right legs move together. The pace is slightly faster than a walk but slower than a canter or gallop.

ancestry
The breeds from which a horse or pony originates. Certain traits, such as body type, height, and strength, are passed on to a horse based on their bloodline.

Blaze

appaloosa
Different types of spotted coat patterns that appear on some horses and ponies, usually ones related to the Appaloosa breed. These patterns include snowflake, blanket, and leopard.

barrel
The main body area in the middle of the horse or pony that holds its rib cage and major internal organs.

bit
A metal bar placed in the horse or pony's mouth between their front incisors and back molars. It attaches to the reins and helps riders to control their mount.

bloodline
The ancestral line of a horse or pony that indicates breeds to which it can be traced.

breed
A group of horses or ponies with a similar bloodline that share common traits and characteristics. Usually, this begins when a foundation stallion mates with a mare to create offspring with deliberately selected qualities.

breed registry
An official record created by certain organizations to document, manage, and monitor the development of a specific breed. Like a stud book, these registers must investigate the parentage of a foal to confirm that it is an official member of the breed.

bridle
The part of the horse or pony riding equipment that goes around the horse's head. The reins attach to this piece to help direct and control the horse.

carriage
A horse-drawn, wheeled vehicle usually pulled by two or four horses. It was predominately used to carry passengers before the Industrial Revolution (1760–1840). Some people still use a carriage for leisure and entertainment.

chariot
Two-wheeled military and racing vehicles pulled by teams of horses in ancient times.

coat
The hair that appears all over a horse or pony's body in various colors and patterns. Not only can it change pattern and color as the horse gets older, but it will also adapt to the weather by becoming thicker in colder months and shedding in warmer months.

Carriage

coldblood
One of the three names used to indicate the temperament of a horse. These types of horses are usually larger draft horses with a calm temperament.

cross-breeding
Combining two or more different breeds of horses or ponies through mating to create a hybrid offspring.

destriers
The horses used by medieval knights to fight in wars.

draft
Work that requires pulling large loads. Some breeds of horses, especially coldbloods, are better built for this type of work because of their strength and build.

dressage
Competitions where horses and ponies are tested on their ability to complete a series of dance-like movements at increasing levels of difficulty.

driving
The act of a horse or pony pulling a vehicle, such as a carriage or wagon, that is guided by a driver for either leisure or sport.

equestrian
Describes all things related to horseback riding, including riders.

equid
Any mammal that belongs to the equidae family, of which the horse is a member.

eventing
A competition where horses and ponies are tested based on their dressage, showjumping, and cross-country skills. The scores are totalled to find a winner.

extinction
When a particular breed, either within a family or species, dies out and no longer exists.

feathering
The long hair that appears on the lower half of some horses' and ponies' legs. There will be more or less hair across this area depending on the breed.

feral
A term that describes horses or ponies that have not been domesticated and, instead, remain running wild.

fetlock
A joint with a tuft of hair on the back of the leg. The hair can be short or long.

flea-bitten
A coat pattern of small, gray, or brown flecks that some horses and ponies develop as they move from youth to adulthood.

foal
A young horse or pony, usually within its first year of life. The males are called "colts" and the females are called "fillies."

foundation sire
The earliest male member, or stallion, of a genealogical family that a breed can be traced back to.

gait
The sequence, rhythm, and speed at which a horse moves its legs. Also known as the footfall pattern.

grazing
The consumption of grass or gorse on pasture land. Since horses and ponies are natural herbivores, this roughage makes up a large part of their diet.

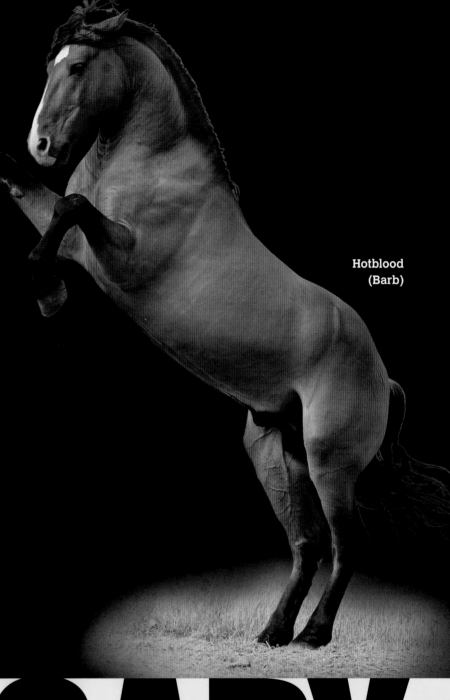

Hotblood
(Barb)

GLOSSARY

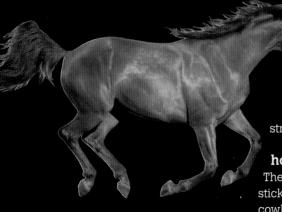

Gallop

hands
A measurement used to indicate the height of a horse. One hand equals approximately 4 in. (10 cm).

harness
The equipment used to attach a horse or pony to a vehicle for pulling. It is made up of many parts, including the collar, reins, and shaft.

harness racing
A type of racing where two horses are attached by harness to a cart, called a sulky, and raced over a particular distance for speed.

heavy horse
Coldblood horses typically used for heavy activity. Calm and sturdy, these breeds are popular draft

herd
A group of horses or ponies that live together. The term can be used to describe both kept and wild.

horses, but are also commonly used for farm work.

hoof
A keratin-covered structure that is part of the foot.

horn
The part of a Western saddle that sticks up at the front. It is used by cowboys to tie cattle.

horseshoes
Rounded, metal shoes that farriers fix to the bottom of the hooves. They stop the keratin on the hoof from wearing down.

hotblood
One of the three names used to indicate the temperament of a horse. These types of horses are usually athletic horses with a more excitable temperament.

hybrid
Two or more different breeds of horses or ponies combines through cross-breeding.

jockey
A professional racehorse rider that is hired by an owner or trainer to ride one of their horses in a race.

lasso
A rope tool with a noose on the end used by Western riders to catch horses or cattle.

light horse
Hotblood and warmblood horses typically used for "light" activity. Athletic and spirited, some breeds are popular racing horses, while others are commonly used for cattle driving and eventing.

mare
The crest area of a horse or pony's neck where hair grows.

mount
A rideable horse or pony of any breed. It can also refer to the act of climbing onto an horse.

muzzle
The part of the face of the horse that includes the chin, mouth, and nostrils.

packhorse
A horse that carries heavy loads on their back, usually navigating difficult terrain.

paddock
An enclosed, outdoor area where horses are sometimes kept.

pasture
An area of land with grass and other plants that can be used for exercise and to graze a horse.

pinto
Different types of patched coat patterns that appear on some horses and ponies, usually ones related to the Pinto breed, in two different colors. These patterns include tobiano and overo.

purebred
Horses and ponies bred from parents of the same breed.

ranching
The act of running a farm, called a ranch, that

Miniature horse

specializes in breeding and raising livestock.

reins
A piece of leather that attaches to the bit part of the bridle to help a rider control the horse or pony.

rodeo
Sporting competition where cowboys exhibit their skills in various events such as bronc riding and barrel racing. The competitions are usually associated with the American West.

saddle
A type of seat that attaches to a horse or pony to give riders better support and stability. Saddles reduce strain on the horse's back.

Different types, such as Western and English, are used in different parts of the world,

semi-feral
A horse or pony that has not been domesticated, but still occasionally interacts with humans.

show jumping
Competitive events that individually test horses and ponies based on their ability to clear jumps of varying heights at high speeds.

solid colors
Describes horses and ponies with only one color apart from face or leg markings. The four most common solid colors include chestnut, bay, brown, and black.

stable
Enclosed barns with stalls, called stable boxes, used to house horses and ponies.

stallion
An adult male horse or pony that can be used for breeding.

stamina
The ability to exert energy over a long period of time without great tiredness. Horses, especially coldbloods, are famous for this skill.

Steeplechase

GLOSSARY

Team of 33 horses pulling a cutting and threshing machine

steeplechase
Racing competitions that require horses to jump over multiple obstacles (usually fences) at high speeds. It is also sometimes called "jump racing."

stirrups
The part of the saddle that supports a rider's feet, allowing them to go faster. Different types are used in different parts of the world, such as in Western and English ridding.

stock
A shortened version of the word "livestock," which refers to a herd of farm cattle. Stock horses and ponies are often used to herd these animals.

stud
Farms that specialize in breeding horses. The breeders that own the farm can either receive horses or ponies or send their own to another farm for mating.

studbook
A register of purebred horses used to document, manage, and monitor the development of a specific breed. Like a breed registry, the parentage of a foal must be confirmed to be an official part of a breed. Most are "closed," meaning that only foals with two parents of the right breed can be resisted.

tacking up
The process of equipping a horse or pony before riding it.

Warmblood (Morgan)

This includes putting on its saddle, bridle, reins, harness, and bit. Different types of tack are also needed depending on the length and pace of the ride.

temperament
The character of a horse or pony. Different types of horses and ponies will act differently based on the characteristics of their breed. For example, hotbloods and warmbloods are known for being more spirited and exciteable, while coldblood horses are famous for being calm and docile.

trekking
A horse or pony ride over a long, difficult trail. Today it can often be done by hire at various national parks around the world.

undercoat
A protective layer of hair on a horse or pony that grows underneath the outer layer. The density of it keeps horses and ponies warm in cold conditions.

warhorse
A horse used for the purpose of war. Throughout history, horses have played various different roles in major wars, but are generally no longer used for this purpose in most places around the world.

warmblood
One of the three names used to indicate the temperament of a horse. These types of horses were created by crossing hotblood and coldblood horses to create calm, athletic horses that are both sturdy enough for heavier work but agile enough to move quickly.

withers
A muscular area above the top of the shoulder blades at the highest point of the back. This is the point from which all horses and ponies are measured.

GLOSSARY

INDEX

A

"airs above the ground" 92–3, 94
Akhal-Teke 42–43
Alexander the Great 41, 137, 139
  Bucephalus 41
American Civil War 61, 62–3, 192–3
American Indian Horse 67
American Quarter Horse 11, 17, 36, 50–1, 66, 68, 89, 115
  American Quarter Horse Association 89
American Quarter Pony 123
American Saddlebred 17
American Shetland Pony 122
American Standardbred 10, 57, 64–5
  Cambest 64

Hambletonian 10, 64
American Warmblood 67
American West 19
Amish 64, 151, 174
Andalusian 39, 46, 66, 76, 96–7
  Blanco 97
Anglo-Arab 34
Appaloosa 17, 36, 68–9, 81, 115, 123, 145
  Chianti 145
Arabian 17, 31, 32–3, 34–5, 36, 38, 47, 57, 86, 91, 101, 115, 119, 131, 137, 163, 165, 167
  El Badavi 86
  Shagya 34
  Smetanka 106
Arabian Horse Show 101

Araboulonnais 165
Ardennais 165, 166–7, 180
Ariégeois pony 129
artillery 63, 76, 159, 160, 167
Australian pony 143
Australian Stock Horse 110–11
Auxois 165
Azteca 66
  Casarejo 66

B

Barb 38–39, 74, 96, 101, 131
  Spanish Barb 39
Bardigiano 139
barrel racing 73
Bashkir Curly 128
Batak pony 137
Battle of Antietam 192
Battle of Mühldorf 158
bedding 185, 187
Bedouin 32–3
Belgian Draft Horse 151, 168–9, 170–1, 174, 175
  Big Jake 151
Belgian Warmblood 104
  Big Ben 104
  Berbers 38
  Bidet Breton 160
  bits 59
  Black Forest Horse 178
blinkers 150, 153
books 8, 120
Bosnian Mountain Horse 129
Bosnian War 129
Botai 175

Boudicca 41
Boulonnais 165
  mareyeur 165
Brabant 180
braiding 153, 154, 195
breed registries 11, 67, 88–89, 98
  American Stud Book 89
breeding 10–11, 17, 21, 31, 32, 34, 35, 42, 49, 77, 79, 86, 88–9, 98, 99, 104, 112, 125, 126, 130, 131, 135, 138, 139, 143, 146, 147, 153, 154, 161, 164, 165, 169, 179
Breton 160–1
  decoration 160
  Heavy Draft 160
  Postier 160
Brumby 26
Budyonny 109
Budyonny, Marshall 109
bullfighting 66, 97
butteri 47, 115
Byerley Turk 44

C

Camargue horses 24–5, 26
Canadian Mounties 48–9
carriage driving competition 61, 119
carriages 17, 49, 105, 109, 145, 147, 162, 170–1, 174, 181, 196
cart racing 64, 151

American Quarter pony

Criollo

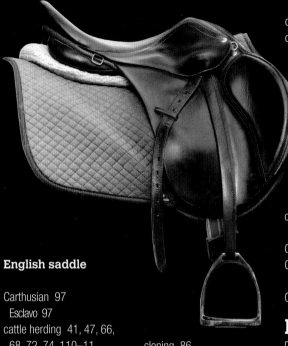

English saddle

Lipizzaner

Jutland heavy horse

INDEX

Oldenburg

**Medieval drawing
of a horse skeleton**

Vladimir

INDEX

ACKNOWLEDGMENTS

Photographs ©: 123RF: 159 top right (Daniel Prudek), 177 right centre (Ewa Mazur), 119 right upper centre (Gilad Fiskus), 122 top right (Kseniya Abramova), 159 top left (Luisa Vallon Fumi), 159 top (Luisa Vallon Fumi), 140-141 spread (Luke Wilcox), 172 bottom (Mads Hjorth Jakobsen), 205 right (Mads Hjorth Jakobsen), 48-49 spread (Mark Spowart), 81 bottom right (Martina Osmy), 90 bottom right (photogearch), 101 left centre (Pierangelo Roberto); Alamy Images: 39 top centre (Buddy Mays), 112-113 (Chris McLennan), 101 bottom left (David Fracassi/Pacific Press), 100 (Juniors Bildarchiv GmbH), 79 bottom right (Mammals, Alius Imago), 41 bottom centre (Serg Glovny/ZUMA Press, Inc.), 101 bottom right (Split Seconds); Dreamstime: 35 bottom right, 93 right bottom (Accept001), 35 bottom left (Agamarcyniuk), 175 top, 175 center (Alexander Solentsov), 29 centre left (Amit Rane), 160 top right (Andreykuzmin), 34 center left (Anke Van Wyk), 195 top centre (Anna Cvetkova), 67 top right (Anolis01), 175 center left (Aynur Shauerman), 98 bottom left (Azahara Perez), 38 bottom left (Aziz Rimi), 134 top right (Betty4240), 69 centre right above (Bronwyn Mack), 121 bottom centre (Carlos Ramos), 26 bottom left (Carol Hancock), 93 right centre below (Cata37), 131 bottom right (Charles Gibson), 73 centre right (Charles Rausin), 61 right centre (Chinook203), 154 top (Chris Lofty), 36-37 spread (Chris Van Lennep), 29 centre right (Christian Degroote), 97 bottom centre (Ciolca), 179 top (Claudia Steininger), 115 centre (Claudio Balducelli), 173 bottom centre (Conny Sjostrom), back cover top center left (Cynoclub), 145 top centre (Cynoclub), 180 bottom left (Daniel Rajszczak), 45 right centre below (Daniela Jakob), 90 top right (Daniela Simona Temneanu), 73 centre bottom (Danny Raustadt), 124 bottom left (Daria Medvedeva), 40 (Davide Ferdinando Precone), 128 bottom left (Dawn Young), 29 centre far right (Demarsimo Creations), 93 centre (Deymos), 69 top right (Donna Kilday), 59 top right (Dpimborough), 46 bottom right (Dr Ajay Kumar Singh), 71 right centre left (eastern light photography), 109 centre (Edoma), 33 centre (Ekaterina Druz), 186 top (Elena Elisseeva), 39 centre left below (Elena Titarenco), 45 right top (Ellesi), 10 (Enriquecalvoal), 189 lower centre right (Fabien Monteil), 59 centre (Filedimage), 128 bottom right (Fotokon), 139 top centre (Gabriel Robledo), 133 bottom left (Gail Johnson), 68 top centre (Gavril Margittai), 29 bottom left (Ghm Meuffels), 47 bottom left (Gianni D'orio), 41 centre (Gianni Marchetti), 136 centre right (Graham Taylor), 34 bottom left (Gutescu Eduard), 137 bottom right (Gwmb2013), 187 lower centre right (Hank Frentz), 142 top left (Hel080808), 90 top left, 105 bottom right (Hvat10), 64 centre bottom, 108 bottom left, 108 centre (Inna Kudasheva), 80 bottom left, 104 top right, 153 top right (Isselee), 123 top left (Jana Š⊠igelová), 89 left (Janian Mcmillan), 174 (Jeffrey Hutchinson), 153 centre right above (Jenny Bowden), 99 bottom left (Jhernan124), 134 bottom right (Jlcst), 115 top right (Joe Sohm), 187 top right (John Stone), 64 centre below (John Wollwerth), 123 bottom left (Jonathansphotos), 69 centre right below (Joy Mennings), 1 (Juniors Bildarchiv GmbH), 46 top right (Kalnenko), 64 centre right above (Ken Wolter), 85 right (Kevin Quin), 59 bottom right (Kim Christensen), 115 centre (Konstantin32), 91 right centre, 109 top right (Kseniya Abramova), 175 center right (Kutizoltan), 186 bottom (Liza Tishankov), 91 top right, 145 bottom right (Loshadenok), 35 top right (M. Rohana), 167 bottom right (Madrabothair), back cover top right centre left, 92-93 spread, 204 right (Marinko Bradasic), 143 bottom centre (Mark Andrews), 45 bottom centre (Martin Applegate), 163 bottom centre, 165 top left, 167 bottom (Martina Berg), 73 top right (Michael Turner), 73 bottom left (Mikael Males), 42 top centre (Mikle15), 108 top right (Nicole Ciscato), 187 top left (Nigolub), 142 bottom left (Nikol Senkyrikova), 187 bottom right (Notwishinganymore), 59 left centre (Oleksandr Rostunov), back cover top left center left, 31 bottom right, 42 centre, 42 top right, 42 right centre below, 64 top right, 78 centre, 96 centre, 96 top right below (Olga Itina), 49 bottom right, 59 bottom left, 84 top right, 104 bottom, 105 top right (Olga Rudneva), 59 right centre (Patricia Dubbeldam Wezel), 29 bottom right (Paul Brennan), 105 bottom left (Pfluegler), 41 bottom left (Philip Bird), 177 top centre (Ralligeller), 122 left (Robert Crum), 201 right (Robert Young), 104 left (Rolf52), 78 bottom right (Roy Pedersen), 102-103 spread (Rushour), 73 centre left (Russell Stewart), 39 centre left (Ryhor Bruyeu), 160 bottom (Saintho), 52-53 spread (Samrat35), 165 top right (Samuel Areny), 45 right centre, 161 bottom (Sonya Etchison), 169 bottom (Sophie Dauwe), 120-121 spread (Steve Cole), 176-177 spread (Stockr), 50 top right (Stocksnapper), 64 centre above (Suvilli), 91 left (Tamara Didenko), 107 bottom centre (Tamas Kolossa), 45 right bottom (Tanya Yurkovska), 155 left (tbernardstudio), 172 right centre (Thes2680), 147 top right (Thomas Vieth), 163 centre right above (Tony Bosse), 129 top centre (Trafford Photography Limited), 180 bottom right (Turfantastik), 147 centre left (Val Armstrong), 92 bottom left (Ventura69), 38 right, 39 centre right, 39 top left, 47 centre right, 96 top right, 180 top right, 199 (Viktoria Makarova), 81 centre right above (Virgonira), 73 centre right above, 195 top right (Voyagerix), 34 right, 106 top right,109 bottom left,109 bottom right,131 centre,173 bottom right (Zuzana Tillerova),123 right centre, 203 left (ZZizar); Fotolia: 81 centre right below (annebe), 138 bottom left (Antje Lindert-Rottke), 119 top right (Archivist), 139 centre right (CallallooAlexis), 191 right top center (chelle129), 99 top left (Christophe Daviot), 55 bottom left (Clarence Alford), 66 bottom left (Gerardo), 69 bottom right, 203 right (hemlep), 163 centre above (jorisvo), 65 whole page (Kaja Sarrapik), 98 bottom right (kristina rütten), 160 center (Laurent Vicenzotti), 67 top centre (Mannaggia), 54, 99 right centre, 206 left (Mark), 86 bottom right (Michael Ireland), 30-31 spread (Neil Johnson), 84 bottom (zuzule); Getty Images: 169 right, 208 (anakondasp), cover (Fabio Petroni), 94-95 spread (Leon Neal), 44 bottom left (Print Collector), 160 top right (traveler1116), 158 (ZU_09); iStockphoto: 26 bottom right (Ababsolutum), 135 right top (akaplummer), 79 top left (albanwr), 186 left centre (alex_west), 191 centre upper (alexxx1981), 153 centre bottom (Andrew_Howe), 135 right centre above (andylid), 145 right centre below (Andyworks), 80-81 spread (artofMomentS), 200 left (Ashva), 33 top left (AsyaPozniak), 150-151 left (AtWaG), 187 centre main (Bill Chizek), 124 bottom right (Binnerstam), 126-127 (BirgitKorber), 156 center (Blulz60), 27 bottom right (brytta), back cover bottom left (Callipso), 89 centre right (catnap72), 167 center right (Cloudtail_the_Snow_Leopard), 194 centre bottom (cmannphoto), 144-145 spread, 200 right (cynoclub), 55 bottom centre, 55 top right (dcdebs), 130 top right (Dickidub), 8 bottom centre (DimaBerkut), 191 centre lower (doubtfulneddy), 153 top centre right (dpe123), 18-19 spread (Drazen_), 8 top centre, 11 bottom right, 32 centre, 92 bottom centre (duncan1890), 133 bottom right (edevansuk), 185 lower centre right (Elenathewise), 143 bottom right (evaeisenlohr), 22 top right (falun), 195 lower centre right, 195 bottom right (FooTToo), 16 3/4 spread (gadagj), 39 bottom (gebut), 101 top right (George-Standen), 66 top right (Gerardo Aguilar Ortiz), 125 top centre right (glaflamme), back cover top right, back cover left, back cover top left center right, back cover bottom right, back cover top left, 12-13, 23 bottom right, 68-69 spread, 81 centre bottom, 135 right bottom, 152, 162 (GlobalP), 42 centre right (grebeshkovmaxim), 195 centre right (Greggors), 191 centre left, 196-197 spread (Groomee), 27 centre right (gyro), 185 lower right (Harlequin129), 23 upper right, 161 top (htrnr), back cover left centre (ilbusca), 121 right centre below (Isaju), 133 centre above (Isla Hampson), 125 bottom (jacquesvandinteren), 125 top right (Jared Stine), 71 centre (Jarin13), 26 centre right (jeangill), 134 centre, 135 centre (Jennifer Sanerkin), 121 right centre (Joesboy), 137 centre (Jules2013), 144 bottom left (Julesru), 23 lower right, 43, 70 centre right (Julia_Siomuha), 187 top centre (justhavealook), 185 centre (kerkla), 32 bottom left, 51 centre, 87, 190 left (Kerrick), 33 top right (kiekje), 105 bottom centre, 153 bottom right, 167 top right (kondakov), 21 centre (labetti), 33 centre right (labrlo), 122 bottom right (LaVonna Moore), 129 centre right (lbcphotographer), 44-45 spread, 81 top right, 145 right centre, 147 bottom right, 147 top left (LOSHADENOK), 151 centre (LostINtrancE), 22 centre right (magical_light), 6-7 spread, 23 main centre, 42 right bottom, 191 top left (mari_art), 175 bottom left (MarkSwallow), 17 bottom right (Marta_Kent), 188 main (martinedoucet), back cover left centre lower (matthewleesdixon), 78 top right, 133 top right (mauinow1), 136 centre bottom (MikeLane45), 23 top right (Mindy Musick King), 195 right main (Mordolff), 195 upper right (Mur-Al), 51 centre right below (NastjaPungracic), 161 left (oceane2508), 161 top center (oceane2508), 2-3 spread, 51 centre right, 116-117 spread, 181 right, 191 bottom centre, 207 right (olgaIT), 4-5 spread (ozgurdonmaz), 9 (PeopleImages), 17 centre, 198 right (Phooey), 32 top right (pifate), 148-149 spread, 182-183 spread, 198 left (pixalot), 135 right centre below (ProjectB), 14-15 spread, 185 upper centre right (purple_queue), 17 top right (Radiokukka), 119 bottom right (Raylipscombe), 185 upper right (republica), 184 3/4 spread (rterry126), 121 top right (sbonk), 80 center frame, 101 centre (seraficus), 19 bottom right (Sjo), 50 bottom right (Smsl_photography), 42 right centre, 98 top right (Somogyvari), 21 bottom right, 115 right centre (SoopySue), 50 bottom left (stevecoleimages), 163 top right (steverts), 118-119 left (Stitchie), 137 top left (StratosGiannikos), 125 top centre (subtik), 151 bottom right (theasis), 162 bottom left (THEPALMER), 187 upper centre right (Timbenh), 191 top right (tirc83), 20 (tom_kolossa), 119 centre (traveler1116), 115 centre right (undefined undefined), 24-25 spread (USO), 188 centre (vmenshov), 32 centre right (VUSLimited), 93 right centre above (wingedwolf), 194 centre lower (winhorse), 11 top right (Yerbolat Shadrakhov), 73 centre right below (Zuberka), 51 top right, 71 bottom centre, 146 (Zuzule); Library and Archives Canada: 133 centre below; Library of Congress: 192-193 spread (Alexander Gardner), 170-171 spread (Carol M. Highsmith), 4 left, 17 right lower centre, 22 centre left, 61 top left, 62-63 spread, 64 centre left, 68 bottom left, 89 centre, 115 bottom centre, 119 right lower centre, 151 upper centre right, 151 lower centre right, 153 top centre left, 162 top left, 175 bottom, 175 bottom right, 202 left; Bryn Walls for Scholastic Inc.: 163 center left; Shutterstock: 153 centre left (1000 Words), 129 centre left (2HB2hb), 59 bottom far right (Ad van Brunschot), 41 bottom right (Al.geba), 71 right bottom right (Anastasija Popova), 57 top right (Andrzej Kubik), 114 (Arina P Habich), 21 bottom left (Bene_A), 131 top right, 164, 165 bottom, 177 right centre below, 179 center, 179 bottom (Bildagentur Zoonar GmbH), 34 centre right (CatwalkPhotos), 110 centre (Catzatsea), 115 bottom left (ChameleonsEye), 111 (Christopher Meder), 97 bottom right (cornfield), 176 centre (cristalvi), 129 bottom right (Crobard), 145 right top (cynoclub), 163 bottom right (Daniel Requena Lambert), 131 bottom left (Dave Green), 169 top (defotoberg), 186 centre (Delpixel), 22 bottom right (Dennis W Donohue), 145 top left (DragoNika), 168 (E. Spek), 154 right (eastern light photography), back cover top center right, 163 centre right below, 195 centre (Eric Isselee), 17 right upper centre (Everett Historical), 41 top right (GoodWin777), 188 top (Gorlov-KV), 56 bottom left (Gregory Johnston), 67 bottom left (Grigorita Ko), 189 top left (Groomee), 86 centre left (Hannes Vorhauser), 191 bottom right (hedgehog94), 55 bottom right (Horse Crazy), 28 (Jacek Sledzinski), 72 (Jeanne Provost), 110 bottom right (jennifer and champy), 189 bottom right (Josep Curto), 71 right centre right (Joss Chan), 181 bottom left (Julia Shepeleva), 188 left (kaband), 169 center (Kartouchken), 138 top right (Katho Menden), 86 top right (kovop58), 69 bottom centre (Lenkadan), 93 top left (Leonard Zhukovsky), 60-61 spread, 202 right (Lisa Kolbenschalg), 107 top right (Magda Munteanu), 124 top right (Magnus Binnerstam), 55 right centre, 154 bottom (Makarova Viktoria), 61 right top (Melissa E Dockstader), 71 right bottom left (Melory), 132 (MichalDobes), 39 top right (Morphart Creation), 177 right top (mRGB), 45 centre (Neil Roy Johnson), 110 bottom left (Neubs), 178 bottom (Nicole Ciscato), 71 right centre middle (nikoniano), 71 right bottom top (NiP photography), 107 bottom left (No:veau), 155 right (OlesyaNickolaeva), 46 bottom left (Olga_i), 173 top left (Onyx9), 110 top right (opailin), 57 centre left (Osetrik), 59 bottom centre, 204 left (Pavlo Burdyak), 130 centre (Peter Turner Photography), 115 centre left below (PROMA1), 189 upper centre right (Raksha Shelare), 194 centre left (rokopix), 56 centre right (Rolf Dannenberg), 186 left bottom (RukiMedia), 161 bottom center (sainthorant daniel), 29 centre (Sergei25), 147 right centre below (SF photo), 189 top right (sharon kingston), 153 centre right below (skmj), 58 (sunsinger), 125 top left (Susanne Fritzsche), 97 left (Taras Verkhovynets), 166 (tatianaput), 88 (Thomas Kelley), 61 right bottom (Tyler Olson), 86 centre (venars.original), 186 left lower centre (ver0nicka), 147 bottom left (Vera Zinkova), 71 centre left (Viktoriia Bondarenko), 130 bottom left (Wildpix productions), 142 top right (Wirat Suandee), 61 centre top (Yard 1509), 70 bottom, 97 top,106 bottom (Zuzule); The Granger Collection: 69 top centre; Wellcome Collection: 13 top, 13 bottom, 151 top right, 190 center left, 190 center, 190 center right, 190 bottom, 206 right; Wikimedia: 79 bottom left (Amandajm), 139 centre left (BS Thurner Hof), 178 top (Carl Steinbeiber), 159 center (Comanche Warrior Lancing an Osage, at Full Speed, artist: George Catlin/Smithsonian American Art Museum/Gift of Mrs. Joseph Harrison, Jr.), 147 right centre above (DanDee Shots), 89 bottom centre right (David Ohmer), 27 top left (Discasto), 60 centre left (Dunton's Spirit of the Turf Magazine/Ealdgyth), 89 bottom centre left (Handicapper), 57 bottom right (Harvey Barrison), 55 centre inset (Jean), 163 top (Jim Legans, Jr), 85 bottom left (Jon Kassel), 61 centre bottom (Just chaos), 106 centre left (Keep-Smiling), 47 top left (Kent Pledger), 120 bottom left (Leonard J. DeFrancisci), 66 bottom right (Luis H. Saldana), 176 bottom left (Michael Gäbler), 81 centre top (Mogens Engelund), 139 bottom right (Natalia), 159 bottom left (National Library of Scotland/Knochen), 80 centre (Niels Simonsen), 128 centre (Silar), 143 top left (Tanaka Juuyoh), 167 top (The Grande Armée Crossing the Berezina, artist: January Suchodolski/Piotrus), 121 top left (United States Coast Guard, PA2 Christopher Evanson), 159 bottom right (USMC History Division/Rhoades/KMJKWhite), 21 top right (Shonagon/test2).

Belgian Heavy Draft